HANS HOLZER'S
PSYCHIC
YELLOW
PAGES

Other books by Dr. Hans Holzer

HANS HOLZER'S
PSYCHIC YELLOW PAGES

THE VERY BEST PSYCHICS, CARD READERS, MEDIUMS, ASTROLOGERS, AND NUMEROLOGISTS

HANS HOLZER, PH.D.

CITADEL PRESS
Kensington Publishing Corp.
www.kensingtonbooks.com

CITADEL PRESS books are published by

Kensington Publishing Corp.
850 Third Avenue
New York, NY 10022

Copyright © 2001 Aspera Ad Astra Inc.

All Kensington titles, imprints, and distributed lines are available at special quantity discounts for bulk purchases for sales promotions, premiums, fund-raising, educational, or institutional use. Special book excerpts or customized printings can also be created to fit specific needs. For details, write or phone the office of the Kensington special sales manager: Kensington Publishing Corp., 850 Third Avenue, New York, NY 10022 attn: Special Sales Department, phone 1-800-221-2647.

First printing: October 2001

10 9 8 7 6 5 4 3 2

Printed in the United States of America

Library of Congress Control Number: 2001092059

ISBN 0-8065-2302-6

CONTENTS

PREFACE

As the new millennium begins, there seems to be renewed interest in things paranormal. For a while, when times were really good, fewer people looked for a psychic fix. But it is a fact that whenever the real world goes to pieces, or into a downward spiral, some people look for voices from beyond in the hope that the gifted ones will tell them that things are bound to get better soon.

What makes the quest different this time around is the considerable progress the world has made through techno-logical marvels and accomplishments that were simply part of science fiction not so long ago. As people seem to accept that we can actually plan to explore far-off galaxies before long and discover how the mind works and how life begins, it does not seem so far-fetched to think that maybe, just maybe, some clever people can bend the space-time continuum and reach out into the tomorrow that is not yet or across the miles into territory beyond the horizon.

Today, fewer conservative scientists scoff at the idea of extrasensory perception, psychokinesis, and distant viewing, astral out-of-body experiences, and healing beyond the bound-aries of known medicine. They grudgingly admit that maybe the whole subject ought to be worthy of real studies as long as they are undertaken by scientific rules. Unfortunately, that is not always possible: What makes the paranormal possible is precisely that it does not proceed by normal rules. So the next best thing we can offer is competent, unbiased, reasonable observation—in other words, the quest for evidence to go with findings of a paranormal kind. And that, my friends, is exactly where I stand.

This is a book meant to be wholly practical and independent in its judgment. It takes the point of view of the "consumer," the person consulting a psychic or other professional diviner or card reader—people who are essentially fortune-tellers.

I hasten to add that I am not referring to so-called "gypsy fortune-tellers," a term usually inferring dishonesty, which is a great disservice to the Romany people, who are neither fortune-tellers nor dishonest. But there are some such dishonest "readers," some of them real gypsy people, and some not, and there are always victims.

Follow the commonsense rules in this book, and you will not be one of them.

Part I

THE PSYCHIC WORLD: HOW REAL IS IT?

1

How to Define
a Psychic

The gift of being psychic, or being a psychic "reader," a medium, a clairvoyant, or whatever term is used to describe a practitioner of the art of divination, depends upon a force within that person that Prof. Joseph Rhine of Duke University called extrasensory perception, or ESP for short.

Some people possess more of this energy force, some less, but it is neither miraculous nor "supernatural" in nature; it is merely puzzling to those who cling to the belief in a universe that can be perceived only by using the ordinary five senses. Such limitation does not allow for psychic phenomena, and when they do, they must be explained in some other fashion consistent with a limited view of the universe. Of course, the explanations do not work. The entire range of observed or experimentally induced psychic phenomena defy the traditional view of our world and cannot be squeezed into the narrow parameter of our ordinary five senses.

But in order to understand what a psychic is and does, one needs to understand what exactly extrasensory perception (ESP) is to begin with.

THE SIXTH SENSE

ESP may be defined as the ability by individuals to obtain information beyond the limitations of the time-space continuum. In simple terms, the ability to perceive something one couldn't possibly perceive under known laws of cause and effect must be attributed to a different phenomenon, a different power than the one ordinarily in operation with the so-called five senses.

ESP phenomena are part of "mental" phenomena. Psychic research divides phenomena into mental and physical phenomena. Mental phenomena include clairvoyance, clairaudience, clairsentience, telepathy, and psychometry. ESP is the driving force in all of these. The "physical" phenomena, principally trance and materializations, do not come under the heading of ESP phenomena but ESP may be present in all such manifestations. The driving force in physical phenomena, however, is psychokinesis, a physical force, rather than the purely mental force responsible for ESP phenomena.

Clairvoyance is the ability to "see clear," that is, beyond the boundaries of time and space. It applies equally to seeing into the future and seeing into the past. It also applies, of course, to seeing into a distance away from oneself and observing occurrences going on either simultaneously, in the past, or in the future. Some phenomena of this kind involve both distance in time and space, others merely one of the two.

Clairaudience is the phenomenon of hearing sounds, such as voices, not emanating from visible sources in the immediate vicinity of the percipient. Auditory phenomena may be from the present, from the past, or from the "future"; they may occur in the immediate vicinity of the observer or over a long distance. Phenomena of this category may be a combination of several possibilities. The incidence rate of clairvoyance is much higher than that of clairaudience.

Least frequent is the phenomenon called clairsentience, one form of which is the registration of specific scents for which there appears to be no logical reason. These scents represent associations both with people and with places and in this manner communicate certain meanings to the percipient. They may be from the past, present, or so-called future, or they may be from a distance, just like the other three forms of ESP. However, due to the limits imposed by the nature of odors, clairsentience alone is not significant in the understanding of material and is usually a secondary manifestation along with clairaudience or clairvoyance. However, it follows the same channels and is activated by ESP precisely the way clairvoyance or clairaudience is.

Psychometry is the ability to derive information from touching objects. This is based on the theory that emotional events create a thin film that coats all objects, including people, in the immediate vicinity of the occurrence. This coating of objects or people is permanent and does not dissipate, except in a very minute way of little significance to us in our lives. A psychometrist coming in contact with such objects or individuals will be able to read the coating substance and thus will be able to reconstruct the emotional event. Most psychometry concerns the past, some of it bears on the present, and occasionally psychometric readings pertain to the so-called future. Some individuals need to touch an object that has been on the person of one who is about to be investigated, while others get stimuli from being in the immediate vicinity of the person, without touching him. Psychometry has been used successfully to locate lost persons, with the medium touching an object belonging to the lost person and reconstructing his immediate past. In some as yet little understood fashion, inducing agents such as personal possessions may also result in projections into the future of the owner, thus making psychometry useful in crime prevention and other branches of detective work.

Telepathy, or mind-to-mind communication, is probably the best-known form of ESP. It works primarily between living people but is certainly the base of alleged communications with the dead as well. Telepathic thoughts or images are transferred from one mind to the other. The message is encoded, sent through space at great speed, received by the mind of the recipient, decoded, and brought to consciousness. The entire process is almost simultaneous. Since we are dealing with tiny amounts of electromagnetic energies actually transmitted through space and thus traveling from one person to another, some "time" must elapse, but the amount of time is so infinitesimal that it appears to be simultaneous transmission. More than any branch of ESP, telepathy is capable of inducement, that is to say, willful attempts to make it work. In many ways it resembles radio transmissions. The strong desire of the experimenter to succeed is frequently sufficient impetus to make the telepathic communication succeed. Depending upon the relationship between sender and receiver, the communication may be partial or complete. The closer the emotional ties between the two individuals concerned, the more likely that the results will be satisfactory. "Being in tune" is not a mere figure of speech, but a very real condition enhancing telepathic communication.

The difference between clairvoyance in the present, even at a distance, and telepathy is slight. The two forms of ESP overlap. However, clairvoyance is never induced, always spontaneous, while telepathy can be induced or planned. When telepathy is spontaneous, that is, unexpected, it differs from clairvoyance in that thoughts are being transmitted from another mind. With clairvoyance, visual imprints are received; in clairaudience, spoken words or noises are received, but in telepathy thoughts are received.

Man is either asleep or awake. The sleep state represents roughly one-third of the time spent on the physical plane. In the sleep state the bonds of consciousness are loosened and the ties between conscious and unconscious minds are sometimes very, very slight. In this condition, it is easier for telepathic material to enter the unconscious mind of the receiver than when he is awake. Consequently, much ESP material enters the receiver during the sleep state. The advantage of this entry is that the obstacle of the conscious mind is removed, thus more of the message can be absorbed. The disadvantage is that, upon awakening, the receiver may forget part of the message, or personal dream material of a symbolic or psychoanalytic nature may intrude upon the ESP material, become mixed up with it, or in some way alter the purity of the impression. We do not have much control over the way we receive ESP material from others; to send material while asleep has thus far proven to be impossible.

Despite some extraordinary happenings indicating a close relationship between thoughts and actual physical action, ESP does not make people act in certain patterns or cause things to occur. Indirectly, ESP may cause people to receive certain thoughts or impulses and then react to them, but we do not have the power over others via the ESP route the way hypnotists may temporarily hold power over a hypnotized subject. ESP is both a power and channel of communication. It has many facets and forms of appearance, and it works best on the unconscious level. What makes it operate is similar to electromagnetic current, and it thus depends upon a sufficient supply of that energy in the sender, and to a lesser degree in the recipient.

Like all psychic force, however, frequent use of ESP powers does not deplete the individual but in some as yet not fully understood way helps replenish the supply of psychic energies. The more we use ESP, the more we have. Above all, ESP is not a miraculous power given to a few chosen ones; ESP is not something you can buy or acquire in mind-study courses alone; it is a natural facet of human personality inherent in everyone, frequently left dormant because it is not always fully understood. Its development should be taught in schools the way the three R's are, and perhaps in the not-too-distant future it will be. Whatever else ESP may be, it most certainly is not *super*natural.

SEEING WHAT'S TO COME

Perhaps the most tantalizing aspect of ESP is its application to the foretelling of future events. It stands to reason that nothing interests a person more than to know what lies ahead, whether for himself, for the community in which he lives, for a loved one, or simply in terms of general world conditions. The forbidden is always most attractive. Forbidden in this respect does not mean that there attaches anything evil or unsavory to foreknowledge of the future, nor does any religious faith forbid it. What references there are in the Bible to mediumship, generally based upon misinterpretations or mistranslations of ancient Greek terminology, refer to the consulting with mediums rather than the talent of foreseeing the future. The prophets of the Old Testament were held in high esteem and the gift of prophecy was always held to be divinely inspired.

Nothing matters more than knowledge of what lies ahead, since it covers conditions that have not yet come to pass so that there is the possibility of preparing for them in one way or another. Knowledge of contemporary events, even if they transpire at a distance in space, are less dramatic. True, Swedenborg told his audience of the great fire at Stockholm while hundreds of miles away and while the fire was actually going on. The effect was most dramatic, but his audience also realized that there was little if anything they could do about the event itself and it would take some time before the truth of Swedenborg's statements could be confirmed. As it was, he had been entirely correct in his visionary experience.

Delving into the past and describing conditions with which one is not normally familiar may be related to the ability to foretell the future in terms of technical procedure, but in terms of human interest it does not rank as high as the quest for tomorrow. This is, of course, simply due to man's greater interest in what lies ahead than that which has already become part of his experience. Quite definitely, we cannot alter past events. We may be able to change our attitudes toward them, but that implies personal changes rather than changes of events that have already transpired. We may be able to make some adjustments to events while they are going on, such as news of an earthquake occurring at a distance out of expectation that it may eventually hit us also, but in general the only area where we can take action based upon ESP foreknowledge lies with the ability to foretell future events.

There is still another aspect that makes the ability to foretell future events more controversial and tantalizing than any other aspect of ESP. An event that has not yet come into being is something that the ordinary person cannot perceive or even conceive, something that does not exist and has no reality. Yet, hundreds of thousands of people are able to describe in great detail situations and happenings that come to pass only at a later date. If this is true—and research has amply borne it out—then our concept of time and the sequence of events are subject to revision. Quite clearly, if people in significant numbers can foresee and foretell future events far beyond the law of chance and far beyond guesswork or generalities, then either our sense of time is wrong or the events themselves are predestined by some superior law with which we are not yet fully familiar. It is very difficult to judge such matters from within the same dimension, and it is quite impossible for anyone to be totally outside it at any time. One must therefore construct a theory that would satisfy the existence of many such experiences pertaining to the so-called future, while at the same time satisfying our basic

three-dimensional concepts of life on earth and the established view of the time-space continuum. I will examine the
nature of time in a later chapter, but for purposes of this
aspect of ESP, let it be stated that time is a human convenience, adopted in order to have a reference point; events are
indeed predestined to a large degree by a system that I prefer
to call the Universal Law. About this also more anon.

Precognition is the ability to know beforehand, to have accurate information about events, situations, and people ahead
of the time that we become consciously aware of them. The
majority of precognitive experiences occur spontaneously and
unsought. Some people may have an inkling of a precognitive
situation shortly before it occurs by feeling odd, experiencing
a sensation of giddiness or tingling in various parts of the body
or simply a vague foreboding that a psychic experience is about
to take place. To others, these things come entirely out of left
field. Many find the ability to foretell future events more of a
burden than a blessing because they begin to believe that foretelling bad events may in some way be connected with their
causing them. This, of course, is not true. By tuning in to the
existing conditions and through ESP picking up that which
lies ahead, the receiver is merely acting as a channel without
responsibility to the event itself, the outcome, the timing, the
result of the event, or the moral implications of it. He has no
more control over what he foretells than a radio set has control over programming coming through it. I have letters from
people who think that they are "evil witches" because they
foresaw an accident or death of a friend or loved one and then
it happened exactly as they had foreseen it. They wonder
whether their thoughts caused the event to occur, especially in
cases where there was an unpleasant relationship between the
psychic and the victim. There are cases on record where
thought concentrations may have caused people to be influ-
enced at a distance, may even have made them do certain

things that were not consciously in their will, but this requires a conscious and deliberate effort, usually several people working together, and lacks the spontaneity of ESP flashes generally associated with true precognitive experiences.

Actually, the ability to look into the future is in every one of us, starting with primitive instincts, when man senses danger or love or warmth and reacts accordingly. Through intuition in which his inner voice warns him of danger or somehow vaguely makes him react with caution against dangerous individuals or situations, to the higher stage of the "hunch" where actual ESP begins. A hunch is a basically illogical feeling about a person or situation that influences one's thinking and actions. Following a hunch means to go against pure logical reasoning. If the hunch turns out to be correct, one has had a mild ESP experience. If the hunch turns out to be false, it may not have been a hunch at all but fear. The two are very much alike. Fear of failure, fear of a confrontation that is undesirable may frequently masquerade as a hunch. The only way to tell the two apart is the sense of immediacy, the sudden appearance and the short duration of the true hunch, whereas fear is a lingering and generally somewhat extended feeling.

Beyond the simple hunch there lies the ability to foresee or foretell actual events or situations. This ability is called precognition, meaning foreknowledge. Whether the foreknowledge is of events that occur one minute later or a year afterward is of no importance. The technique involved is exactly the same since we are dealing here with a dimension in which time, as we define it, does not exist.

The precognitive process goes through a variety of stages or degrees. There is, first of all, the situation where one foresees or foretells an encounter with either a situation or a person without "getting" any specifics as to time and place, mainly receiving only the basic message. When this simple precognitive experience occurs in the dream or sleep state it may be surrounded by, or couched in, symbolic language, in which case parallel situations may well masquerade as the message itself. For instance, you may have a precognitive dream about your brother having bought a new car that he wants to show you. The following day there is a phone call from him advising you that he is going to visit you in the near future. When he arrives, it turns out that he has just remarried and wants you to meet his bride. The car of the dream experience was the symbol for the new wife. In the waking condition, however, descriptive material is much more precise, and even though not every precognitive experience contains the desired details of time, place, and description, the absence of the material from the unconscious mind allows the message to be much clearer and more precise.

Next comes the precognitive impression where a time or place element is included; this may be only partial, such as a numeral "flashed" above the face of someone who appears as a precognitive vision. Or it may be a key word spoken by an inner voice that relates to the circumstances under which the precognitive experience will take place. Depending upon the individual personality of the receiver and his state of relaxation at the time of the experience, the precognitive message will be either partial or complete. If the material is merely routine although of some emotional significance to the receiver, it is less likely to contain dramatic descriptive material than if we are dealing with catastrophes, warning of dire events, or precognitive material of importance to more than one individual. Those who are able to foretell plane crashes, for instance, which is a specialty among some clairvoyants, do so with a great deal of detail. Fires and earthquakes also seem to evoke graphic response in the ESP consciousness of those able to foretell them.

The curious thing, of course, is that not all such occurrences take place as predicted. This, however, is not due to the inaccuracy of the vision or precognitive experience, but to the total lack on the part of the visionary as to correct judgment of the time element, coming as it does from a timeless dimension. There remains the question whether the person with ESP ability foresees the future around a specific individual or independent of that individual. If a number of precognitive predictions are made about one individual by a number of seers independent of each other, then the future event must cling to the aura or electromagnetic field of the individual about whom the predictions are made. If, on the other hand, individuals foretell such events in the future about an individual without being in that individual's presence, then a channel into the future itself seems to have been opened in which the individual who is concerned with those events merely plays a part and a part over which he has no control.

Anyone doubting the factuality of precognition need only consult the records of psychical research societies throughout the world for detailed descriptions of cases, carefully recorded by them over the years.

SEEING WHAT WAS

Just as the future does not yet exist when viewed from the present, so the past is no more when seen from the same vantage point. Although artifacts may be standing from distant periods in the past, the past itself is gone. The events shaping it and the people in it are no longer in existence in the physical sense of the word. There is one basic difference between the past and the future. The future has no evidence in terms of the ordinary five senses. The past, on the other hand, has existed already and therefore does leave evidence of having been at one time.

The difficulty in coming to terms with these expressions lies not so much in the limitations of our ordinary five senses as in the terminology we are forcing ourselves to use. By dividing our consciousness into three distinct segments—past, present, and future—we are arbitrarily cutting a steady flow of consciousness into separate and distinct units. In actuality, the progression from past to present to future is continuous and uninterrupted. It is also relative to the observer, that is to say the present of now becomes the past of now plus one. The past is nothing more than the present gone on. In essence, past, present, and future are made of the same stuff. The dividers are artificial and flexible. The only proof that something has become objective reality, that is to say has already happened, comes from observation of the event. If we were not there to notice it, the event itself would transpire just the same, even though there would be no witnesses to record it. When we thus speak of the past, it is to be taken as subjective in the sense that it is the past as seen from our individual points of view. These individual points of view may be similar among most people, but they are nevertheless nothing more than the sum total of individual observations and reflect the past only because the observers are at a later juncture in time than the observed event. Perhaps it would be more correct to speak of such events as accomplished events rather than past events.

By contrast, future events could be characterized as unrealized events. The reality of the events would be identical; only their relationship to the observer would differ. From the point of view of the observer, past events have occurred and can no longer be altered. Future events, on the other hand, exist independently but have not yet occurred in relationship to the observer and may conceivably be altered, at least in some instances.

There are several ways in which we can actually transport ourselves, or anyway parts of ourselves, into the so-called past.

In psychometry we derive impressions from an object, from a person, or from a place about events that have taken place sometime before our experiment. These impressions are always emotionally tinged. Purely logical material does not seem to survive. The outburst of emotional energy whenever traumatic events occur furnishes the raw material with which objects, people, or places are coated and which contains the memory banks of the events themselves. In touching an object or person or being in the immediate vicinity of the event, we are merely replaying it the way a phonograph replays a prerecorded record. The events themselves do not possess any active life and the reproduction is quite faithful, subject only to the limitations of the transmission and the personality traits of the receiver. Therefore, the message may contain part or all of the original event, it may come through correctly or partially correctly, or it may be a mixture of event and personal interpretation, since, after all, the receiver is human and not a machine. But the process itself is basically an impersonal one; it should work equally well, no matter what the occasion or where the location of the experiment is.

In psychometry, then, we read a kind of emotional photograph of past events. In reconstructing it through the psychometric impulses and with the help of our conscious mind, we are not actually re-creating the event itself but merely an imprint or copy of it. This, however, is sufficient to derive information about an event and thus learn facts that may otherwise be lost in history. Some years ago, in a book entitled *Window to the Past,* I showed how a medium can be taken to historical "hot" spots, places where puzzles in history have not been fully resolved, and attempt psychometry to resolve pending issues. Mrs. Sybil Leek was thus able to pinpoint the actual location of Camelot in England and of the first Viking landings on Cape Cod in Massachusetts. ESP in this application is a valid and very valuable tool of historical exploration and can undoubtedly be used much more than it has been in the past, when all other means of historical research fail. To be sure, the information obtained in this manner is by no means used verbatim to correct missing parts of history but is used only as a departure point for research in conventional ways.

A second method of visiting the past is astral projection, also called "out-of-body experiences," in which our inner self, the etheric body, leaves the physical abode temporarily and travels, usually at great speeds. Ordinarily, astral projection is in space rather than in time. It is, however, quite possible to direct one's astral projection into a predetermined segment of past history. It works better if done at the location one aims to investigate, but can also be done a distance away from it. The success will depend upon the power of visualization by the subject, and the absence of interference from conscious or unconscious sources. Induced astral projection should not be undertaken alone but only in the presence of a competent observer. The subject, who should have a history of past astral travel, will then suggest, or have suggested to him, that travel into a particular region of space and time is requested and that all the information obtained once one gets there should be recalled upon return and awakening. Somewhere on the borderline between astral projection and psychometry lies what the late Eileen Garrett called "traveling clairvoyance." In traveling clairvoyance part of the medium is projected outward and is able to observe conditions as they existed in the past without actually leaving the physical body. This, however, is a talent found primarily in professional mediums and those with a great deal of experience in controlling their phases of mediumship. It is not an easily acquired talent. In any event, astral projection is accomplished by lying on a comfortable surface, preferably at a time of day when the body is reasonably tired and relaxed, and by gently suggesting an outward motion of the inner etheric body. Closing one's eyes while suggesting to oneself the loosening of the bonds between conscious and unconscious minds initiates an outward floating, which will eventually become a physical sensation. The inner self may leave the physical body through the upper solar plexus, at the top of the head or through the stomach area. Return is accompanied by a sensation of rapid deceleration, experienced as a kind of free fall, a spinning and occasionally unpleasant feeling of having fallen from great heights. This, however, is due only to the rapid change of speed between the etheric body and the physical body. The adjustment is undertaken in a comparatively short time and can therefore be momentarily unpleasant, but is in no way representative of danger to either body or mind.

Hypnotic regression, as it is used in connection with reincarnation research, also propels the individual into the past. Such experiments, always undertaken under the supervision of a professional hypnotist trained in parapsychology, may result in the obtaining of information from past incarnations and can be verified independently afterwards. With regression it is always best to suggest to the subject that the past memory will not be retained upon awakening in order to avoid any traumatic residue. Thus, the only information about the past available to the researcher is that which the hypnotized subject brings while in the hypnotized state. Since hypnotic regression is more concerned with personal experiences in past lives rather than with historical exploration, the thrust of the investigation is somewhat different from that required for purely past-oriented research.

There are a number of instances on record where people have accidentally entered a "time warp," that is to say areas in which a different time stream was still extant.

One such case concerns a young man who drove from northern Oregon to California and suddenly found himself at the bend of a road in a blizzard, although he had left in August when the weather was extremely hot. For what seemed to him a full day he found himself in a mining town among people dressed in clothes of the early 1900s. He remembers vividly having spoken to them and found them to be three-dimensional people. Suddenly he was seized by panic and, regaining the safety of his automobile, drove away, to the bewilderment of the entities he left behind. Shortly afterward, he found himself back again in the present and the relative comforts of a hot August day.

One must not classify such experiences as hallucinations, even though hallucinations are possible with certain individuals. With cases of this kind, the material obtained during the incident is the crux of the explanation: in the case of the young man, detailed descriptions of his encounter seem to indicate that he did indeed enter a time warp of sorts. Whether this was due to his own mediumistic abilities or to the location at which he encountered the phenomenon is difficult to assess. But similar cases have been reported from time to time where people, and even vehicles, from the past have been observed amid contemporary scenes, only to vanish a few moments later or to return on other occasions or to other observers. Scenes from the past are not unlike ghosts except that ghosts are tied to specific locations and personal fates whereas these scenes seem to exist independently and encompass a variety of individual people within them. Why some of these scenes from the past "hang around" while the majority have faded away, we do not as yet know. In all cases known to me, however, there have been emotional connotations involved, and I thus feel that unresolved emotional problems may be at the base of keeping such scenes in existence. Perhaps someday we will devise an apparatus to replay historical occurrences at will.

Albert Einstein has pointed out that energy cannot dissipate but must continue to exist even if it is transmitted or otherwise changed in form. Could it not be that the emotionally tinged scenes, which, after all, represent energy, exist in a dimension not ordinarily accessible to us for observation? On occasion, however, specific individuals are able to penetrate into this dimension where past events continue to move on a different time track from the one we have created for our own convenience.

Thus, walking into the past is both a matter of choice and a matter of accident. Either way, the past is far from dead and continues to intermingle with our present. Probably the most common form of "reading" the past history of a person or a place is the kind of ESP that permits one to tell facts about such a person or a place without having access to any information or any previous conscious knowledge of the person or place. Since this is a very common talent, it must be assumed that the past continues to exist all around us, that is to say exudes tiny particles of itself so that those sufficiently sensitive to it may derive information from the emanations.

2

What to Do and Not Do When Consulting a Psychic

The first step in learning about the various forms of psychic activities is to consult directories such as this one or listen to word of mouth, which in this field is particularly significant. But finding the appropriate person to consult is only half the job. If the reader is to derive full benefit from such an association, he or she should know how to behave, what to do and what not to do, and how to evaluate the result of such encounters. One of the greatest problems in this field is not the large number of frauds operating in it, because that number is very small; rather it is the uncritical attitude of the individuals consulting the professionals coupled with a false expectation on the part of many, that makes it so difficult to speak of universally acceptable results.

To begin with, a medium or whatever psychic practitioner one consults is only an intermediary between some information or a personality, allegedly deceased, and the one seeking this information or person. The first thing to forget is that notion that the professional consultant is some sort of supernatural being, possessing powers that in themselves are capable of changing the world, performing seeming miracles, or otherwise behaving in contradiction to natural law. In earlier centuries, mediumship was frequently considered a gift of God, denied to other human beings, and it gave the one who exercised it the aura of the supernatural. Sometimes this led to near-religious worship of psychics; sometimes the very same psychics were accused of being in league with the devil.

In the days of the Old Testament, prophets were considered extraordinary human beings somewhere between man and God, certainly not ordinary citizens. Christianity has tended to make mediumship either a saintly device, in which the mediumistic personality speaks as a vehicle of God, or a diabolical instrument, in which case the messages coming from the medium are to be considered evil. Christianity hasn't been able to place mediumistic individuals into a category of their own, to accept psychic phenomena as natural forms of human consciousness. Nearly every other religion has ascribed special attributes to people capable of functioning as psychics, ranging all the way from inspiration to divinity. Sometimes the mediumistic individual is referred to simply as a master, at other times the medium is possessed by the deity itself, but the notion that mediums could simply be people with a particularly high degree of sensitivity to vibrations carrying thought energies has not found acceptance in any religious establishment.

It is only in the light of today's scientific understanding that mediums are properly classed as individuals with greater sensitivities than the average. We know that the dividing line between sensory perception and extrasensory perception is thin and flexible indeed, and that being mediumistic is by no means unnatural or "supernatural."

It is well to remember this and not to approach a public reading or sitting with a sense of awe but rather with a healthy curiosity and a balanced approach that allows neither for extreme skepticism nor for uncritical belief. Always remember that the person giving the psychic reading, or the

astrologer or numerologist or whatever, is a professional performing a service as well as he or she can, that the practitioner may fail at times and succeed at others, that he or she
may be good with one person and not good with another,
and that, in sum total, you are dealing with a fellow human
being not so much different from yourself.

If you have chosen a particular practitioner to consult,
make sure you do not give more than your name, and not necessarily your real name. I have often tested mediums by giving
a fictitious name, only to find that the really good ones will get
my actual name in the course of the sitting. I recall the late
Lillian Bailey of London, of whom I had heard a great deal. In
order to make sure that the test would be adequate, I refrained
from communicating with her directly, but asked the editor
of the *Psychic News* to make the arrangements for me. Mr.
Maurice Barbanell, the editor, thereupon called Lillian Bailey in
my presence, asking her to arrange for a sitting with a certain
Mr. Wood, for whom he could vouch. This was necessary as
mediums are sometimes harassed by newspaper reporters dis-
guising themselves as believers, or even an occasional police-
man trying to stir up trouble.

After I had arrived in the suburban home of Lillian Bailey
and had taken a seat opposite her, she went into a deep
trance, and her control, a Scottish doctor, took over her
speech mechanism. Within a matter of three or four minutes,
this control exclaimed: "Why, you are not Mr. Wood at all.
Your name is Hans Holzer." Needless to say, I was surprised.
A hostile reporter would assume that the editor of the *Psychic
News* had informed Miss Bailey of my true name, but such
was not the case, because Mr. Barbanell was as scrupulous in
his work as he was reliable in his integrity.

Nothing would be lost if you were to give a false name, if
that is your desire. On the other hand, if your name is of little
meaning to a stranger, there is no need to lie. In my case,
disclosure of my real name would automatically disqualify any

material concerning my published career. In the case of an ordinary or average individual, little is likely to be known to the medium consciously, and if in making the appointment no address is given, even the remote possibility of a dishonest medium's checking up on a prospective sitter would be eliminated. In all the years I have tested mediums, I have never met a medium who went to the trouble of checking up on a sitter's personal circumstances. It is true that Spiritualists maintain cards concerning regular visitors to their camps and that these cards are frequently passed from one medium to another in a fraudulent manner. But the material on these cards is obtained in routine sittings, and no one goes out of his way to collect a file on individual sitters for the sole purpose of defrauding them.

Very few psychics can do a full reading without sitting opposite the client, especially the first time. On occasion, I have been given bits of information of a psychic nature on the telephone by such renowned mediums as the late Betty Ritter or by Ethel Johnson Meyers, but that I think is due to the fact that we have sat together many times and that a permanent link had thus been established beforehand. On first acquaintance, a personal visit is always recommended. People who would like to take the easy route of obtaining psychic readings by mail (or telephone) are only deceiving themselves. Those who dispense such readings without prior personal contact are either extraordinarily gifted mediums or unusually cynical. You should never tell the reader why you are seeing her or him, only ask for a sitting. It is a common and unfortunate mistake to book a psychic for consultation and then to go into the reasons for the consultation. It is understandable, especially if the reasons are compelling ones or emotionally motivated, but in doing so, the client removes a large element of believability from the resulting material.

Once an appointment has been made, it should be kept, and kept on time. Reputable psychics apportion their time very carefully because they can do just so many readings a day. Otherwise, they might endanger their health, and if not that, at least their accuracy. Psychic work requires physical energy, and that energy must be replenished through rest and sleep in order to be readily available at full strength. Some mediums can do as many as ten to fifteen readings a day, half an hour each, only to fall exhausted at the end of the day. Others take but a single client a day. It is difficult to set norms for such work, as every medium knows his or her own strength. Probably the safest number of readings per day lies somewhere between two and six.

Whether you are going to the residence of the psychic reader or expect the reader to come to yours, the etiquette is the same. One should be as relaxed as possible, ask permission if a tape recorder is to be used, and should not smoke, unless encouraged to do so by the medium. Incredibly, some mediums do smoke and rather heavily, although it is essentially not conducive to their work. But then one of the best and most evidential psychic healers preceded his work with extreme sexual activities, which he believed supplied him with the necessary "fuel" to perform his work.

It is not only all right but useful to exchange a few generalities with the psychic reader, especially if it is the first time that you have met him or her. This relaxes both parties and sets up a vibrational bridge between reader and client. The voice serves as a link, regardless of what is being said. Naturally, the conversation should not contain leading material that would be brought up during the actual sitting. The initial conversation, which should not last beyond three or four minutes, can concern itself with the weather, with the difficulties or lack of same in reaching the place for the sitting, or it can touch on psychic research in general, books one has read, and so on. Personal business should be kept out of the conversation.

By the same token, beware of the psychic who asks personal questions right off the bat. A reputable medium will not ask questions, she or he will make statements that the sitter can either accept or deny. Among Spiritualist mediums there have been a number of those who thrived on seemingly innocent questions that supplied them with the bulk of their "psychic information." Such deceit was possible only with the collaboration of the naive sitter, of course. A sitter who does not answer leading questions is not likely to be deceived.

On the other hand, once the sitting begins, and most psychic readers or mediums will give their clients a sign that they are getting "into" the sitting, full attention should be paid to everything that is coming from the lips of the psychic. If the reader is merely a clairvoyant, using personal psychic abilities to give the reading, information will be coming forth almost immediately. If the psychic is of the Spiritualist persuasion, there may be alleged communications from spirits supplying the medium with information he or she gives to the sitter. In the case of trance mediums, a control will first speak through the entranced medium, announcing himself or herself, and frequently this will be followed by discarnates speaking directly with the sitter through the medium. In the latter case, it is permissible for the sitter to reply.

When the psychic practitioner speaks as herself or himself, giving information obtained through ESP, the sitter need only take notice. At times, the medium may ask confirmation or denial of a statement made. If that is the case, it is quite sufficient to say, yes, no, or maybe. Any elaboration beyond that while the sitting is still in progress is self-defeating.

On the other hand, once the sitting has been concluded, the sitter should feel free to comment upon the accuracy or lack of same displayed by the medium. But even then it should be kept in mind that the sitter might wish to return for another session at some future date. Consequently, the information disclosed by the psychic practitioner at this first meeting and confirmed by the sitter might become a repetitive element the next time, in which case it no longer has any

evidential value whatsoever. Therefore, when additional sittings are contemplated by a client, extreme paucity of words
and cautious confirmation should be employed, sufficient to
reassure the medium that he or she has done a good job but
not sufficiently elaborate to furnish the medium with information that he or she could use consciously or unconsciously
in future sittings. This does not mean that the medium may
do this fraudulently, but that the medium's unconscious
mind may pick up information in this manner that will reap-
pear on future occasions.

At times, a psychic may be unable to make the necessary
contact, perhaps because a sitter is too "cold," that is, has put
up a defensive shield knowingly or unknowingly, or because
of personal circumstances concerning the medium. In order
not to disappoint the sitter, an object will be requested that
will become an inducing agent for the medium to get "into"
the vibration of the sitter. Through psychometry, the ball gets
rolling, so to speak, and the reading proceeds. There are of
course mediums who are strictly psychometrists, who can do
nothing but interpret impressions gained from touching an
object belonging to a certain person.

Psychic practitioners run the gamut from excellent and
evidential to bad, just as human beings differ greatly in their
personalities. A client has a right to demand a certain level of
performance if a professional is being paid for a sitting. A
client should not be satisfied with generalities, well-meaning
pastoral advice, and statements about alleged dead relatives
so vague that they could fit anyone. In particular, names or at
least initials of individuals referred to by the medium should
be demanded, specific circumstances and detailed descriptions
of events alluded to should be requested, and in general a
channeling of the medium's abilities toward a reasonably
accurate description of events or persons should be expected.

The late Eileen Garrett, probably one of the world's greatest mediums, was extremely adamant about poor performance

by "sloppy" mediums. She always insisted that a medium come up with dates and names, detailed circumstances, and evidential material each time out. Her own training by the late Dr. Hewitt Mackenzie of the British College of Psychic Studies had made her into the great and evidential medium she became, and she wanted no less from her colleagues in the field.

The uninitiated sitter sometimes has strange ideas as to fees for psychic work. Some individuals even consider payment for unsuccessful sittings not called for, making the work strictly speculative in their minds. I recall how the late motion picture actress Miriam Hopkins asked the late Betty Ritter to come to her house for a reading. Miss Hopkins was herself highly psychic and also very difficult to get along with at times. I do not know what happened between the two ladies, but apparently Miss Hopkins was not altogether satisfied with the reading given her by the medium. She refused to pay her. When I discovered this, I took into account the work put in by Betty Ritter and the financial status of the movie star and asked her to pay Betty Ritter for her time, whether she liked the reading or not. In some states, for reasons of law, psychic practitioners do not charge for their work per se, but for the time given to a client. After all, a medical doctor does not charge for successful healing, but only for the effort and his time and knowledge. If the doctor fails, the patient doesn't get his money back.

What then is a proper fee? There are those who prefer to go to a public sitting, whether in a Spiritualist church or some other accessible place, a meeting where anywhere from five to fifty people are in the audience, being read individually and publicly. Sometimes, especially with well-known mediums, as many as one thousand fill major concert halls for the sole purpose of receiving messages from their beloved ones on the other side of life. In these cases, a modest contribution of between $5 and $10 is standard nowadays, and though it is called a "free will offering," it is really the expected thing to do. Private bookings run anywhere from $50 to $500, depending upon the medium. Most reputable mediums who have been established because of their evidential performance will charge between $100 and $200 for a sitting, but there are some who will charge more, and there are many little-known mediums of good quality who will give sittings for as little as $5.

What is considered good evidence and what is not? When a psychic reader whom you have just met for the first time tells you some pertinent facts about your own past or present, including names, dates, and situations, and if the majority of such statements are accurate, then it stands to reason that statements made about your future may also turn out to be accurate.

Predictions concerning well-known people or those in the limelight of public attention cannot be taken seriously unless they are very specific. The fact that a certain celebrity may die within the following year is not a psychic prediction but a good guess, considering the person's age. The prediction that someone may try to shoot the president of the United States isn't psychic either; a president is a very likely target for a potential assassin, especially in times of stress.

On the other hand, predictions concerning individuals who are not in the public eye are more likely to be evidential, especially if they are precise and contain names and dates. I have quoted some of these amazing predictions with individual practitioners listed in this book. Evidence then consists of a fair percentage of hits, detailed material come true, and the absence of intensive questioning on the part of the medium. Do not expect a professional psychic to be good each time out, or to be equally as good with your friend as with you. A number of factors enter each reading, and conditions may vary the results a great deal. Mediums, on the other hand, should know better than to give sittings when they are physically low or emotionally upset.

If your quest is not for a psychic reading but for something beyond that, such as a so-called life reading, you should realize that there was only one Edgar Cayce, and as yet no one had come forward to equal his feats. So-called life readings offered by a number of well-meaning and some not so well-meaning individuals, at fees ranging from $20 to $100, contain largely fantasies that cannot be checked out for veracity. Anyone with genuine memories of a previous life will come to realize his previous existence sooner or later through flashes of memory, through recurrent dreams, or through some form of déjà vu. Deliberately seeking out one's former lives, just out of curiosity, invites delusion. Occasionally, reputable mediums may obtain flashes of information about a sitter involving previous lifetimes. Ethel Johnson Meyers, one of the most reputable mediums around, frequently tells a sitter what he did in an earlier lifetime, or why he is going through certain difficulties in this one. I don't doubt Ethel Johnson Meyers's sincerity, nor the source of her information, but it is always difficult to prove such statements in the accepted scientific sense, unless actual names, dates, and situations are revealed that can be checked out.

Don't ask a medium to get in touch with a dead relative, don't induce communications, because you will either fail or fall victim to fraud. If a discarnate wishes to communicate with you for good reasons, he or she will find a way to get through to you. Reasons include the need to demonstrate continued existence in another dimension, unfinished business on the earth plane, or a state of difficulty in your own life that the discarnate relative or friend wishes to help you with. The best way to hope for such a contact is to sit with a competent psychic and open yourself up to whatever or whoever might "come through." A psychic reading is not a telephone communication. You cannot dial the person to whom you wish to speak, you cannot make demands other than to be given a reading containing as much identification and evidential material as the medium is capable of giving.

Another common misconception concerns the ability of the so-called dead to instruct the living in matters of superior knowledge. While it is true that discarnate relatives frequently help those on the earth plane by guiding them, they do so without breaking any of the laws of nature, and are in fact only helping people help themselves. Then, too, it should be realized that humans passing into the next dimension after physical death do not automatically acquire some superior spiritual or other knowledge, but are simply people existing in a dimension in which thought is the only reality. They, too, must learn to live in the new dimension and acquire knowledge that was denied them in their earthly existence. To assume that the spirit person has vastly superior foreknowledge is to delude oneself; on occasion, discarnates are permitted to divulge bits and pieces of information that might prove helpful to the person on the earth plane, but this is always done in accordance with universal law and under the control of the spirit guide supervising the communication. We should realize that the so-called spiritual dimension is as much subject to strict laws and natural conditions as is the denser, physical atmosphere in which we presently exist.

A reputable psychic will give honest readings without editing anything, whether the message is good or bad. This even includes warnings of danger or imminent death, because such knowledge should not be held back if the medium is truly an intermediary and nothing more. However, giving negative messages should be done in a cautious and soothing way, always leaving the door open to the possibility of error or misinterpretation. In this manner, the dire warning becomes merely a bit of foreknowledge with which the sitter is being armed, rather than the unfailing sword of Damocles hanging overhead, about which he cannot do anything.

Sitters should never ask a professional psychic whether they see such and such in their future, or what they think about such and such a person. By mentioning an event or a specific person, or some special characteristic of themselves, and expecting the psychic to render an opinion, they are in fact only looking for an emotional crutch. Such crutches are more properly found among ministers and psychologists, not mediums. On the other hand, if a sitter is anxious about a certain aspect of his life, he may put the question in general terms, without divulging any detail, hoping that the psychic reader will come up with something that fits the situation. If the psychic does, the sitter should take into account the possibility of some thought reading entering the result, meaning that the psychic may very well pick up the sitter's own thoughts and intermingle them with genuine psychic material.

In any event, living one's life by relying upon the opinions and predictions of psychic individuals is a poor way of spending one's time. Ultimately, all decisions rest with us, opportunities being thrust at us by fate. We are free to act, free to accept, reject, or ignore conditions around us, and while we seek the professional services of psychic practitioners, we should not abdicate our decision-making powers to them under any circumstances. If the majority of psychic professionals were infallible, then sitters consulting a number of such practitioners should obtain parallel readings. But they do not. Frequently the readings differ or contain totally opposite material.

Then again, there are many instances on record in which the same information is obtained from a variety of psychic professionals. I myself have obtained proof of the veracity of a number of such statements from half a dozen professional psychics who know nothing of each other or of me. On the whole, however, personal conditions of both sitter and psychic at the time of the reading, interpretations, prejudices, and other as yet not fully understood elements enter a reading, and results will never be one hundred percent identical, even if the same sitter consults a variety of readers.

Ultimately, psychic readings help you to understand yourself better, give you an occasional glimpse of what lies ahead, and above all afford you the chance to be prepared for it when it comes. Readings of this kind also reassure your conviction that life goes on beyond physical death and that those who have gone before you are indeed alive and well and able to communicate with you at certain times and under certain conditions. The world of psychic professionals then complements the world of the living in such a way that it balances it, not replaces it, and the truly happy individual is one who lives his own life in a state of harmony, drawing on both sensory perceptions of the material world and extrasensory knowledge from the next state of existence.

3

AVOIDING FRAUDS

As with every profession, the practice of psychic work
has its categories of people engaged in it for various
reasons. Not all doctors are capable of helping their
patients, and not all lawyers win cases; therefore one should
not condemn a profession already beleaguered by prejudice
and ignorance at times for the ineffectiveness of a few.

Truly great psychics don't advertise. They don't have to:
they are too busy. But there are professional psychics who
have a real gift, and an even greater one of self-promotion
bordering on the unethical at times. There is nothing illegal
in this (at least not until a client makes an official complaint
under the various anti-fortune-telling ordinances) but these
practices do not help the field overall in the public eye.

Making a decent living as a psychic is no less moral than
being a doctor or lawyer. However, good doctors and lawyers
don't send out hard-sell brochures to mailing lists they purchase from professional advertising and promotion agencies
either.

For the past several years, an epidemic of telephone "psychics" has hit the newspapers and tabloid weeklies. Even some
otherwise respectable magazines like *Fate* have succumbed to
the lure of easy advertising money, and never mind their reputation. "Telephone psychics amaze callers with their
powers!" (at $3.49 per minute) screams one ad. "Control

your destiny—readings by LIVE psychic!" (This one is $5 the first minute and $3 each additional minute—and they will keep you on the phone with double-talk and banalities for as long as you, poor sucker, will allow it.) Dozens upon dozens of ads offer readings by psychics billed as "gifted" or by members of the "psychic discoveries network" or a "psychic expert for lovers and family" and so on and so forth. Even a successful singer like Dionne Warwick has headed up a very lucrative television "network" of psychic readers. That one belongs in the same category as those late and unlamented evangelical television ministries interested mainly in their followers' money. As for the actual "psychics" dispensing telephone readings that can run a caller into very large sums: they are neither genuine psychics (though the law of averages demands that once in a while a real psychic might just be among them) nor trained in any way.

Now and then, a 900-number "psychic" will quote a channeling source speaking "through" him, dispensing counsel to the client. Now and then, a genuine psychic, in need of work or cash, will join one of these outfits, and the client really does get something more than generalities for his or her money.

Don't get me wrong: perhaps people like Dionne Warwick and others mean well and have a genuine interest in the psychic field, and may even be psychic themselves. The difference, however, is that the genuine psychics who also do telephone readings, take responsibility for what they tell their clients. They do not defer to a nebulous channeling personality as their source. And good psychic readers give specifics, not pseudo-pastoral counsel; they may not tell the client exactly what he or she wants to hear.

That the usage of the media is part and parcel of this abuse of the genuine psychic work stands to reason. Tabloids, weeklies, neighborhood shopping papers, even some otherwise reputable magazines are only too eager to take the advertising bucks that come with such pearls as "Harness your psychic potential!" "Unlock the mysteries of your destiny!" "Live psychic predictions: Discover your soul mate and destiny now!" "Is evil holding you down?" and, of course, the celebrity endorsements that are supposed to make the promised disclosures of one's great future that much more reliable. Not satisfied with the use of stock photographs of pretty girls, or at least interesting looking ones, to decorate the ads, we are now treated to the pictures (and "presentations") of such celebrities as pop star La Toya Jackson and even former Mrs. Sly Stallone, Brigitte Nielsen, who presents "the next level," to wit, "the Witches of Salem Network" (at only $3.99 a minute). You can buy a lot of broomsticks with that, as long as the calls keep coming.

All this works to the detriment of hardworking established psychics, whose track records speak for them. And ultimately, it works to the detriment of people in need of authentic readings, and, perhaps, a glimpse at some piece of the future.

Judging by the pat answers given callers by the majority of telephone gurus, they must be working from instruction sheets listing certain phrases that are suitable for what the caller will usually want to hear about. Readings received from these 900-number psychics do not perform a useful service any more than 900-number prostitutes and "masseuses" do, though as P. T. Barnum once stated, "there is a sucker born every minute."

Lastly we come to a group of guileless, self-proclaimed metaphysical individuals, who usually come from pretty ordinary and even dull lives. They somehow discover their uniqueness and wish to share it with the masses of believers. More often than not, they claim they have come "from the stars" and are not really like the rest of us earthlings.

Solara Antara Amaa (they also create exotic-sounding names) is big in cosmic consciousness, teaching her own brand of New Age philosophy. Unlike the 900-number vultures, she does no great harm, nor does she offer anything more than a philosophy of her own making. (Those interested in this sort of thing can contact her organization, Star-Borne Unlimited, at 2005 Commonwealth Drive, Charlottesville, Virginia 22901. Telephone 804-293-1111.)

Closely related to channeling is the proliferation of so-called past-life readings. During a past-life session, a psychic will tell a client right off the bat who he or she was in previous lives. Usually, the details of such earlier lifetimes are incapable of being checked out scientifically, as they ought to be, whether the information includes actual names and places or not.

The problem with such easy predictions is that they obscure the very real and highly important research into reincarnation and genuine communications with discarnates (spirits).

As if it were not enough to have to contend with the numerous 900-number psychics, we now have a group calling itself the American Association of Professional Psychics, located in Baltimore, Maryland, which is the brainchild of an astrologer and self-proclaimed psychic named Gail Summer. Now there is certainly a need to sort out the false prophets from the real ones, but I very much doubt that a self-styled association "testing" would-be psychics by having them read for three of their board members is the answer. There is a membership fee, of course, and if the outfit likes the result of these tests, they will "certify" the would-be psychic as fit to enter the lucrative 900-number calling field. Whether this is chicanery aimed at legitimizing the 900 services or whether Miss Summer really has her heart in the right place is a moot question. What troubles me are the qualifications of those testing would-be applicants for psychic work and certifying them as bona fide psychic readers.

By contrast, when I have taken on a gifted individual who is seeking training and testing, as I have done now and again through the years, the tests are many and take several weeks. They range from psychometry tests, readings done for strangers, and visits to allegedly haunted locations. Only after the long-term evaluation of results do we issue a letter certifying that the person involved has performed properly as a psychic reader or medium. There is, of course, the matter of who does the testing and who is really qualified to evaluate the results. After more than forty years in the field, I feel comfortable doing it. The group in Baltimore seems to have links to the 900-number business, according to their taped telephone answer to callers.

My main reason for writing *The Psychic Yellow Pages* is to awaken the average person to the reality of television and telephone "psychics" and to make sure the consumer knows the difference between *them* and the *real* thing.

PART II

THE
DIRECTORY OF
PROFESSIONALS

n this part of the book I list and describe the work of psychic readers, mediums, clairvoyants, metaphysical counselors, healers, or whatever name the practitioners of the art of divination attach to themselves. In parapsychology we like to call them *sensitives*. Some people like to call their psychics spiritualists, especially when the reader is ensconced in a little church of his own, which is very popular since it affords the reader protection from persecution under some of the local fortune-telling ordinances.

Few of these "Reverends" are all that spiritual, but in America Spiritualist ministers do use that title even if they have absolutely no formal religious training.

Whatever term is used to describe their calling, these professional psychics must be judged by their performance records: How accurate have they been in the past? How much specific material are they able to come up with? What are their general working habits and claims? How fair are their fees?

I do not doubt that there are considerable numbers of individuals gifted by nature with the ability to foretell future events, speak of past events or events of which they could not possibly have any knowledge, and to pierce in many ways the conventional curtain of time and space as we have long known it to exist in a world ruled by rational thinking. They do exist, and a fair number among them are extraordinarily gifted; many are good, though not necessarily all the time

41

and with every client; and some are bad, though sincere. Finally, we have the recent phenomenon of "telephone psychics," which I will deal with further on.

Only those personally known to me either through test sittings or long-distance tests, or those whose reputation I have checked up on will be included in this register. Undoubtedly, many practitioners will be left out simply because they were not known to me personally, not because they are necessarily bad.

Furthermore, some of the professionals I met provided photographs of themselves for use in this book. Do not assume that the presence or absence of a photograph is any reflection on the person's level of skill or talent.

These psychics are listed alphabetically, and they may vary in ability and quality of work.

There is also a list of parapsychology societies who may have other psychics in their files, especially in areas not covered in my work. However, it should also be borne in mind that nearly all psychics can do good readings over the telephone, sometimes even of higher quality than in face-to-face sessions. The reason for this is that a telephone reading establishes a line of an electronic nature between the psychic and the client, and that seems to enhance the contact in most cases, thus giving the client a very good reading.

I have had readings from people like Rosanna Rogers and others over the telephone that were detailed and very accurate. This should of course not be confused with the so-called "900 number psychics," who are nothing more than pseudo-readers out for your money. Beware!

Some psychics have declined to give their addresses or phone numbers because they wish to protect their personal privacy.

Lastly, it should be remembered that psychics are people who, like everyone else, have good days and bad days, and who react in different ways to different people, which will influence the results of their work.

4

PSYCHICS

Anderson, Marisa
P.O. Box 5057
Poughkeepsie, NY 12601
Tel: 845-795-1173
www.marisaanderson.com

Marisa is a young woman with careers in advertising, fashion, photography, and modeling behind her. She had exhibited psychic abilities as a child, and her very curious mind and an avid interest in the paranormal eventually led her to develop her psychic gifts.

She is far from the stereotypical image of the medium or psychic reader; her background and education include the Parsons School of Design, the Westchester Academy of Ballet, and even some work as a private investigator. She is fluent in Russian, her father being of Cossack origin. In addition, she is an expert at various sports, including horseback riding, snorkeling, and skydiving.

I first met Marisa at a lecture on parapsychology at a local college, and subsequently worked with her regularly to help develop her considerable psychic skills. She has become very adept with her predictive abilities, and as a medium she has refined her gift to sense both human and animal spirits who have passed on.

I took her to some haunted locations in Manhattan, such as June Havoc's town house, where she correctly described "a girl waiting for a man" (Hungry Lucy and her soldier in the eighteenth century). At Clinton Court she picked up the impression of a high-ranking officer from England around 1780 and "children's games" in the 1830s (a child fell to his death on the stairs and his spirit became a ghost), horses and a carriage (the house was a carriage house previously), and finally, someone named Harry CL—in fact, it was Sir Henry Clinton's place, something she would not have known.

As a reader for private clients, Marisa has had considerable success. For instance, a client named Annie D. was about to look for a used car in the newspaper ads, but Marisa told her not to bother; someone she already knew would soon offer her one. She even described it in great detail. Two weeks later the woman did acquire such an automobile from the mother of a friend.

Bill A. is well aware of Marisa's psychic abilities. On the evening of April 18, 1995, he was speaking to her by telephone when Marisa was suddenly catapulted from the reality of her living room, her eyes fixed on the weather channel map on TV. She psychically saw the state of Oklahoma and was unable to break the vision of a building, sensing that it housed government offices. A van was parked on the street in front of the building, oriented left to right. She asked Bill if the scene was somehow connected to him. It was not, but the next morning the news broke with the story of the tragic bombing of the Alfred P. Murrah Building in Oklahoma City in which many, many lives were lost—twenty-four hours after Marisa's vision.

Marisa's yearly forecasts in January 1996 on WEVD radio were precise. There would be a downed airline flight with the number 8 occurring sometime during June or July, with no survivors. It would leave the East Coast with one stop before reaching its final destination, but it would not make it. It would go into the water soon after departure. She saw a rectangular box to the right and slightly behind the wing area. The plane was a Boeing type. There would be only one who survived the crash itself, but no one would see her in the dark. It would be a difficult case for the investigators, and they would not be able to determine if terrorism or an accident caused the crash.

Marisa's forecast also told of stocks plummeting during the summer, causing intense market concerns; it would seem like a crash!

All of the predictions were eerily accurate. It turned out one woman did survive the crash of TWA Flight 800 and could have been pulled from the water if rescuers had found her in time; the autopsy showed she had drowned!

Marisa was asked about other numbers of the downed plane, but could only get the number 8, and said there were no others. It turned out to be Flight 800—two zeros—and the incident occurred off the coast of Long Island on July 17, 1996. Marisa had "seen" this in January.

Harold G. had an idea to open a store. Marisa accurately predicted that he would open a health-food store in Scarsdale, New York. Within a year he did. She also described a second store in Eastchester, New York. A year later he did indeed open the second store in Eastchester.

Marisa accurately predicted that Ricky, a local hairdresser, would change jobs. She described the location of his new job, and predicted he would later open his own salon on Central Avenue in Scarsdale, New York. This happened exactly as predicted.

A New Jersey graphic designer, Diane C., wanted to know if she would ever meet a man to share her life with. Marisa predicted that within two years she would have a man in her life with a three-letter name beginning with L. Marisa described his build, his unusual facial features and eyes, and even described a wart on the right side of his face. A year and a half later, Lou waltzed into Diane's life exactly as described.

During a session with Cliff A., a computer programmer from New York City, Marisa became chilled, and Cliff gallantly gave Marisa his jacket to drape over her shoulders. When he did, Marisa received some interesting impressions— he would change jobs and move from working with the one who says "all the sardines in Sardinia," and also that he would once again see his old flame, Susan. She also predicted that Cliff, who was then married, would divorce his wife, fight for custody of his three children, and lose. All of this did occur. What transformed Cliff into a believer was Marisa's mention of the "all the sardines in Sardinia," an expression his former boss always used.

What is unique and, at the very least, rare about Marisa's psychic abilities is her gift with animals. She has a unique rapport with pets and is often able to diagnose their illnesses. Sally P.'s cat suddenly became ill for no apparent reason. Marisa touched the cat and told Sally that the cat had been drugged. The veterinarian confirmed that the cat had swallowed some type of pill that had caused her to become ill. Marisa has three cats and four birds, which have no doubt contributed to her great empathy for animals. Marisa is a charming and talented psychic.

Appio, Carol Ann
Flagler Beach, Florida
Tel: 904-439-4215

Carol Ann Appio is one of the very best and evidential mediums I have met in a while. She has a private clientele in Florida but also does telephone readings. She also works with certain official angencies when they are unable to resolve certain problems, which may include important incidents. But that part of her career is not for publication, though I am familiar with some of it.

Before she knew anything about me, except that I wrote

books on psychic subjects, she gave me a spontaneous reading, during which she spoke of films and mentioned the name Dan Fellman. It so happens that Mr. Fellman is the head of distribution at a major motion picture company and someone with whom I have a business connection, as I also write screenplays and produce.

Bard, Ronald
Tel: 914-526-9415
    800-241-2646

Ron Bard is the son of famed trance medium and clairvoyant Yolana Lassaw of New York. Psychically talented, Mr. Bard began his career with individual readings, which eventually led to a cable television show, during which he would give brief readings to callers. Often these readings were accurate.

My own experiences with Mr. Bard include the following: I tested Mr. Bard with objects, and in one particular case he correctly named letters that were concealed inside opaque envelopes without any identifying characteristics on the outside. In this instance he scored with an accuracy that could not be attributed to chance.

Among his interesting predictions were statements made to me: On September 3, 1985, he said there would be "fire and explosions at the World Trade Center" (long before the bombing occurred). He also said I would hear from a lady with whom I had not spoken since 1984, and that her name was Maria; also someone named Thomas was involved. It turned out that Maria did eventually call me again and I consequently introduced her to Miss Thomas, who became a close friend. This happened three years after the prediction.

One of Ron Bard's remarkable talents is his ability to give a reading from studying a photograph. Mr. Bard identifies names, places, and circumstances in his readings—concrete information which allows us to chronicle his accuracy. His many abilities include automatic writing, which is a form of mediumship. Mr. Bard has become a celebrity in Japan and Europe, where he has gained a large following.

Baron-Reid, Colette
Toronto, Ontario, Canada
Tel.: 305-880-0555

Colette Baron-Reid is a busy young woman with a second career as a sucessful recording artist. But her work as a professional clairvoyant is amazingly accurate in terms of details. Though she had never met me before, she was able to pinpoint conditions in my professional life in areas she could not have learned about me from my books. In personal matters, she hit the nail on the head about my relationships and even came up with time frames in which she foresaw that various events in them would materialize. An excellent psychic.

Bassik, Susan
Spiritual Science Center
44 East 32nd Street
New York, NY 10011
Tel.: 212-533-2129

Susan Bassik is the pastor of the Spiritual Science Center. An active minister, she specializes in spiritual coaching and private readings. In her spiritual counseling sessions, Miss Bassik utilizes such tools as meditation, affirmations, and specific remedies to help clients harmonize and attune the spiritual aspects of their personalities.

When I queried concerning her psychic abilities, the following cases were cited.

"When Kathy L., a therapist came for a reading, she was quite upset concerning her financial affairs. I suggested that she learn everything possible about managing money during this time. I told her that by the time she reached forty (she was then thirty-eight) her ongoing financial troubles would be over and she should be prepared to handle large sums of money. One month before her fortieth birthday she received a substantial inheritance. She invested it wisely and was able to look forward to a financially comfortable life.

"Grace J., an executive assistant, was concerned that her son was about to move into a questionable neighborhood— she had been unsuccessful in trying to persuade him to change his decision. During the reading I advised her to go along with his plan since he was trying to assert his independence and the more she argued the more he would resist. Furthermore, I told her that at the last minute something would change his mind. A week later, when the family drove up to his new place, they saw the building surrounded by police. They learned that a burglary was in progress. Needless to say, her son returned home with her.

"Carolyn R., a widow, came for a reading while she was trying to sell her house. A man named Rodney was particularly interested. I told her I was sure he would buy it because the name Rodney came through so strongly. However, they could not reach an agreement on the price and negotiations stopped. A year passed. Though several other 'deals' transpired, none were completed. Late one night my telephone rang and upon answering I heard Carolyn say excitedly, 'It's Rodney! It's Rodney!' Sure enough, another man named Rodney fell in love with the house and bought it on the spot.

"I gave a reading for Pat C., the president of a training and consulting firm, when her business partnership was disintegrating. I told her that her soon-to-be-former partner was no longer interested in the business and if she offered a fair settlement, the matter would not have to go to court. She did this and within two months the business was hers. I also told her that the business would expand into an area she wasn't yet familiar with. This happened the following year. I was able to accurately describe the man she would marry, even though they hadn't yet met. They met and married eight months later.

"Gerald J., a well-known astrologer and author, consulted me when the author of an astrology column in a national newspaper retired. Gerald wanted to take over the column. I advised him that another astrologer had been chosen, but it wouldn't work out. I told him that after six months they would offer him the column, but he wouldn't want it anymore because he would have found something better suited for him. That is exactly what happened."

Reverend Bassik also presides over weddings, commitment ceremonies, funerals, and house blessings and tries to incorporate the vision of the participants in these events. In addition, the reverend teaches a course in chakras for the School of Continuing Education of Marymount Manhattan College. The Spiritual Science Center sponsors a monthly meditation service open to the public.

Cattel
4800 S. Maryland Parkway
Las Vegas, NV 89119
Tel.: 702-798-8448

Cattel has lately acquired a reputation as a very accurate psychic reader in Las Vegas and hosts a radio program on psychic subjects, inviting other psychics as guests. In addition she has a center that arranges lectures on a regular basis.

Cattel once telephoned me for a radio interview in connection with a new book I had written, and while I was answering questions pertaining to the book, she spontaneously gave me a reading that had nothing to do with the content of the book (the subject matter was ghosts and hauntings). Evidently the voice contact on the telephone triggered psychic awareness, and the reading proved to be accurate and in line with what I was planning to do. Many psychics can give telephone readings as long as you are able to keep talking; the sound of the voice seems to be necessary to keep the psychic contact.

Cattel is a valuable source of information for those who reside in localities where a qualified psychic isn't readily available. She observes strict rules regarding professional conduct and would be able to recommend someone of equally high standards.

Char
Tel.: 313-356-5360
    310-876-6301

Using only one name in her profession, Char resides in both her native Detroit, and occasionally in Los Angeles. I first met Char on October 13, 1983, over coffee, and at that time she was unaware of my professional activities.

Char once told me during a reading that a movie would be made called *The Amityville Curse*. What is remarkable is that in 1983 she was unaware that I had written a book on Amityville, and at that point no film companies had yet shown interest in it. This only came about five years later under a convoluted chain of circumstances; a Colorado film company acquired the rights but did not progress further with the project and passed it to a Canadian film company who did make the film, *The Amityville Horror*, based on my book about the Amityville house. She could not have known about these events five years before they happened.

In 1988 she channeled a spirit named Martha (which happened to be my late mother's name), and also mentioned a woman named Elan, whom I met and became friends with more than two years later.

Char is one of the few psychics who actually give names, not only initials or physical descriptions. She has gained a good reputation and frequently gives television appearances. Char is a very personable young woman with a love of horses.

Craig, Pat
P.O. Box 3171
Lithonia, GA 30058
Tel.: 404-978-8100

Pat Craig, a mother, homemaker, and a native of North Carolina, is considered one of the most reliable readers in the Atlanta area. Emotional entanglements and matters of the heart are considered her specialties, even though she is often consulted by business professionals for more mundane reasons.

An experience with near-death phenomena alerted her to a world quite different from that espoused by her Baptist upbringing. An interest in psychic phenomenon ensued and she began to develop her own skills.

In October 1993 Pat informed a client who was distressed over a broken marriage that her husband would return, see her within three days, and eventually come back for good. The husband visited her two days later and returned for good by Christmas, just as Mrs. Craig predicted.

Once, on a whim, a client asked during a telephone reading when she might have news from a friend named Gerald. Without a moment's hesitation, Pat told the caller from Tennessee that she would hear from the man on the ninth of the following month, April 1993. The caller laughed because she had not heard from him in fifteen years! Remarkably, on April 10, he did telephone her.

Actively pursuing a career as a professional psychic when not attending to her domestic duties, Pat has many more stories to her credit.

Daryl, Jason (Lundstead)
2299 North Roosevelt Road, No. 3
Taiban, NM 88134
Tel.: 505-478-2245

Jason Daryl, formerly of New York, presently resides in New Mexico. She is a good psychic with a considerable following.

Deitch, Paula
13554 Rye Street, No. 1
Sherman Oaks, CA 91423
Tel.: 818-501-0269

Paula Deitch gives psychic readings in person and by telephone. She is known to give accurate predictions and utilizes her innate gifts of clairvoyance, clairaudience, and clairsentience to accurately predict events and situations. She advises clients that readings are not "etched in stone"; they should be used to give added insight and perspective to events in their lives, along with their own intuition and desires. She does not give specific time lines, but prefers instead to offer a sequence of events as "signposts" that can lead to given situations. She hopes to illuminate her clients' pathways through her readings so they can fulfill their destinies.

One client, M.K., consulted Paula while she was negotiating to buy a house she very much wanted. As Paula tuned in to the situation, she could see that the house would go to another buyer, but that another house, almost across the street, would suddenly become available and she would purchase this second house. Events happened exactly as Paula had predicted, and M.K. happily purchased the second house.

One evening Paula was giving readings during a party. Paula gave one of the guests a reading and predicted the woman would come into some unexpected money. The guest laughed—however, one month later she telephoned Paula to say that she had won fifty-thousand dollars in a lottery.

During a psychic fair, Paula met Tracy and predicted she would meet a man with salt-and-pepper hair who was her soul mate and life partner. One week later, while working on a job, Tracy did meet a man who fit that description, but nothing came of it. A month later she went to Paula for a reading and mentioned that she had not yet met the man Paula had earlier predicted. Paula tuned in and again advised her that she had indeed met her soul mate, but that the timing was not right (he was already married). Shortly thereafter she reported for an assignment, and the same man with the salt-and-pepper hair was present. This time, though, he was separated, and sparks flew. Today they are together and have a lovely daughter.

With her special talents, Paula Deitch has acquired a good reputation as a reliable psychic reader in the Los Angeles area.

De La Rochelle, Lyn
125 East 87th Street
New York, NY 10128
Tel.: 212-722-9010

Lyn De La Rochelle has been a respected psychic consultant for more than twenty years. Her broad psychic talents include psychometry, interpreting the I Ching, and card readings (she has been using the Enchanted tarot deck for the last seven years), as well as being adept as a Reiki healer and a yogi in the discipline of Paramahansa Yogananda. I have interviewed Lyn and she has recounted some of her successful cases of predictions as follows.

Several years ago G. contacted Lyn for a reading. G., an actress of modest renown, had been offered a major role in an upcoming play as well as a role in a future film. Regardless of her preferences, Lyn's reading showed tremendous success for the play, and thus for the actress. She did choose the play, which became one of the most acclaimed of the nineties, garnering major awards for many involved.

A. went to see Lyn in March, as she was distressed because she and her husband had been unsuccessful in conceiving a child. During her reading, Lyn exclaimed that A. would have what she wanted by the end of the year. A. gave birth to a baby in December of that year.

K., a single mother, was skeptical of finding the right man for a relationship and had given up hope. However, K.'s reading showed something different. Lyn described the man K. would soon meet, a bit younger than she, but attractive, ambitious, and dependable. A week and a half later K. telephoned Lyn to say that to her amazement, she was introduced to the man Lyn had described. Even though it was too soon to tell, Lyn knew that the relationship would be successful.

De Long, Barbara
Tel.: 914-698-8144

Barbara De Long considers herself a spiritualist and was a teacher prior to becoming a full-time psychic reader.

Along with traditional cards, Miss De Long uses special cards she designed and crafted, which will soon be available commercially under the name *Cosmic Deck of Initiation*. The card deck will be accompanied by an instructional manual and interpretations. Miss De Long gives both personal and telephone readings.

DeLouise, Joseph
8 South Michigan Avenue
Chicago, IL 60603
Tel.: 313-332-1841

Joseph DeLouise was a busy Chicago barber when he discovered the gift of prophesy. During the late 1960s he was a truly "hot" psychic, with considerable newspaper publicity, some self-serving, most honestly deserved. Sudden fame gave Mr. DeLouise a feeling of destiny and resulting power as he set out to turn his natural gift into a professional pursuit.

Probably his best-known prediction is his accurate forecast of a West Virginia bridge disaster. Some of his other notable predictions include the following.

After the gruesome Manson murders in 1969 and before the culprits were arrested and tried, DeLouise described one of the murderers as being tall, about 160 pounds, with dark blond hair; the first of the criminals apprehended fit that description. He also predicted that one of the murderers would be in Texas; one of the men was indeed arrested there. DeLouise forecast that September 14 of that year would be important in the case; it was the day that police received their first important clue concerning the Manson "family."

In January 1969 Mr. DeLouise foresaw a tragedy for one of the Kennedys involving water. In July of that year, Ted Kennedy's car plunged off a Massachusetts bridge, killing the other occupant, Mary Jo Kopechne.

Twenty years later, the barber shop long forgotten, this amazing psychic still sees clients. Today Mr. DeLouise also gives predictions regarding the stock market and is registered with the Securities and Exchange Commission as a professional adviser. Stockbrokers use Mr. DeLouise's services to help foresee markets trends so that they can make better choices for their clients.

Doherty, Jane
2325 Plainfield Avenue
Plainfield, NJ 07080
Tel.: 908-757-2508

Jane Doherty, a well-respected psychic in New Jersey, is a regular guest on the popular biweekly Ted Efaw radio show (a call-in program), during which she receives many calls.

As a result of Jane's popularity from her radio appearances, she has gained quite a following of clients requesting consultations. Following are some excerpts and examples from recent readings.

A woman consulted Jane for a reading regarding a knee injury for which an operation had been scheduled. Jane could not "see" the surgery occurring, even though it was already planned, and predicted it would not be needed; she suggested her client return to the doctor for another examination. During the reexamination, the doctor concluded that the previous diagnosis was incorrect and that she did not need surgery to correct the condition. Instead, the woman learned, her knee inflammation was treatable with medication and rest. The surgery was canceled, and obviously Jane's client was delighted with her advice and prediction!

A woman, emotionally distraught over her daughter's long-term alcoholism (over ten years), came to Jane for a reading. The woman's daughter had been in and out of jail and rehabilitation programs to no avail. Jane predicted that her daughter would finally be cured and psychically "saw" that within the year she would move south, probably to Georgia, and while staying there would become emotionally close to a relative. She said that the relative would help cure the daughter's addiction by getting her involved in helping others, and as a result of this transformation she would finally stay sober and create a totally new life in Georgia. In addition, Jane also predicted that the relationship between mother and daughter would be healed. The woman left the reading in disbelief, but Jane instructed her to have faith.

Six months later the woman telephoned to tell Jane that her daughter had become close friends with an uncle, even though they had not had contact in many years. The uncle inspired the young woman to join Alcoholics Anonymous and to help counsel others. The daughter eventually did become a counselor and was able to overcome her alcoholism, and the relationship between the mother and daughter healed— exactly as Jane Doherty had predicted.

During the radio call-in program, a woman telephoned

to ask Jane about her son's health. Her son was scheduled for brain surgery to remove a tumor. The woman explained that the doctor suspected that the tumor was cancerous and to expect complications from the surgery. Jane received an image of the color green as she closed her eyes, then predicted that the tumor would be benign and that there would not be any further complications. She also told the woman that her son would recover from the surgery much faster than expected. Two weeks later, during another program, the caller again telephoned Jane to say that, as predicted, the tumor was benign and there were absolutely no complications.

Once during a reading Jane received the names Ginger and Sydney, and told her client that the names were clues to the future. He would meet someone, and these names would surface around that person. When this situation occurred, Jane predicted, he would understand the meaning and would know his fate. Four or five months later the client telephoned to say he then knew the meaning of the names and went on to explain that he had begun to date a new girl to whom he was very attracted and that her dog was named Sydney and her ferret was named Ginger!

A woman came to Jane for a reading and, during the consultation, received the image of a boat. Jane interpreted the image to mean that the client would go on a boat, probably within six months' time. The woman adamantly answered, "That's impossible! I am afraid of boats and there is no way I'm going on a boat." Jane checked the image again and once again said, "I'm sorry but I still see you on a boat." Six months later the woman again consulted the reader, during which she told her that the previous prediction regarding the boat had been correct. The client went on a vacation with her husband to visit her brother and wife in Florida; the brother had purchased a boat the day before and insisted she take a ride in spite of her protests. She went along. The client related that during the boat ride the only thing she could think of was Jane's prediction.

Once Jane received an image of a log cabin in Montana during a reading for a woman whose husband had passed away several months earlier. Puzzled, Jane told the woman she could not interpret the image and, although she didn't understand it, she felt that the woman's husband was trying to communicate something concerning the log cabin. Jane asked the woman if she had ever been there and, of course, the answer was no. Therefore, Jane surmised it was a clue to the future, that eventually the woman would understand the meaning and then would know her fate.

Several months later the woman returned for another reading and subsequently told Jane how she had come to understand the meaning of the log cabin. A relative of the woman had a boarder living in her house. The relative sold the house and suggested to Jane's client that she take the boarder in as a renter, since the client had extra room and needed the money. She agreed, and within six months she and the boarder fell in love. One night the man revealed that he owned a log cabin in Montana. The woman gasped, suddenly understanding Jane's vision.

Many of Jane's clients return because of the accuracy of her readings. Jane has also done work with haunted houses and ghosts.

Downey, Jim
P.O. Box 11249
Piedmont, CA 94611
Tel.: 800-339-5683
    800-266-5683
    510-658-7792

Jim Downey has a good reputation as a psychic and a healer. He operates a practice in psychic counseling, having had college training in psychology. Not only does he identify his clients' problems, he also tries to help resolve them. In addition to his psychic work, Jim is a teacher of various types of metaphysics.

Several of Jim's cases are chronicled below.

In February 1980, Jim predicted, before witnesses, the failure of an American attempt to rescue the hostages held captive in Iran, and said there would be a loss of American lives. This happened exactly as predicted two months later.

Jim Downey has helped a well-known opera singer afflicted with stage fright; an engineer who was unable to get his designs properly presented; and a teacher who had difficulties relating to people. What distinguishes Jim's healing is that first he identifies the problem psychically, then proceeds to remove it. In each case he has been successful.

One day Jim attended a lecture in Corte Madeira, California. At the entrance desk he met a clerk who complained of having very little energy and of not feeling well. Jim subsequently listed the vitamins and minerals of which she was deficient and predicted this would also be confirmed by her family doctor. The clerk then told Jim she had seen her doctor several days before and he did not mention any such deficiency. Jim told her, "You should hold on to the list because within two weeks you will be told this by your medical doctor." While Jim was awaiting departure at the San Francisco airport, the clerk approached him and related that a week following their conversation her doctor revealed to her that blood tests showed the exact deficiency Jim had diagnosed.

Today Jim Downey hosts his own radio program, which is broadcast on the West Coast and in the Midwest. Jim also works with individuals to identify their previous lives and how they influence their present situations. Jim has a large following for his somewhat unusual brand of psychic insight and healing.

Dratler, Theresa
Tel.: 212-249-7999
     305-673-6993

Theresa Dratler is an articulate, well-educated woman who specializes in tarot card readings and astrology; however, her predominant gift is that of psychic reader.

While consulting her tarot deck, she dispenses advice based upon her interpretation of the cards as dealt. Deborah P., a registered nurse, consulted Mrs. Dratler in 1987 because she felt dissatisfied with her line of work. Mrs. Dratler told the woman during the reading that a career in legal work would be the answer; this seemed unlikely to the client. Nevertheless, the former nurse is now a practicing attorney.

In 1991, a client named Keith C. came to Mrs. Dratler because he did not like his job. The spread of cards indicated to Mrs. Dratler that her client should move to Florida. He did and now owns three retail stores in Miami.

Mrs. Dratler came to me on May 30, 1993, without knowing much about me or my work. She nevertheless gave a very precise appraisal of my feelings, status, and problems—nothing specific in terms of events. Even so, the reading was quite accurate, and the information she detailed could not have previously been known to her.

I saw Mrs. Dratler once more on June 21, 1993. This time she predicted major events for January 1994 in my working life, and she was right. She stated my business relations would be with a Taurus and a Scorpio. That was entirely correct.

Mrs. Dratler has a very unusual way of interpreting the tarot cards; it is unlike anyone else I have studied or interviewed.

While she does not give actual names, she does describe the persons and situations she feels will occur in a client's life, and with me, she was quite accurate concerning things she could not have known. Mrs. Dratler also teaches and lectures on the tarot.

Dykshoorn, M. B.
Tel.: 212-548-3448

Mr. Dykshoorn, a Dutch-born gentleman residing in upper Manhattan, gained fame by helping police in Holland locate missing persons as well as by reenacting murders, which frequently led to solving the crimes.

Dykshoorn is a true clairvoyant and finds the unknown through the gift of "second sight." Mr. Dykshoorn is as far removed from the commercial fortune-teller as can be. He has found buried treasure three centuries after it was buried. His autobiography, *My Passport Says Clairvoyant,* while not exactly a bestseller, is a very interesting study detailing his experience of having the special gift of clairvoyance.

Consulting Mr. Dykshoorn on trivial matters as love and financial prospects is not advised. He would probably reject the request anyway, having psychically detected the nature of the caller's request.

However, those with difficult and important cases similar to the above-mentioned situations will find him very professional, businesslike, and astonishingly accurate. Mr. Dykshoorn has also seriously worked with the parapsychology laboratory at the University of Utrecht in the Netherlands.

Esposito, Peggy
106 West 80th Street
New York, NY 10024
Tel.: 212-877-7345

Margaret Esposito, a personable young woman very knowledgeable in the psychic arts, became aware of her special and unusual gifts at an early age.

When asked to relate her early experiences, she stated, "I became aware that I was different from other children at approximately the age of four. I was able to astrally project myself, 'fly,' 'see,' and communicate with many types of spirit guides and entities. Always having a deep love of nature and animals, I spent my playtime digging up Native American objects in the woods behind my house.

"At the age of thirteen, a friend gave me one of Sybil Leek's books, which explained much of what I have been experiencing over the years. After being nicknamed 'witch' by the other kids, I kept my psychic predictions to myself. I became a studio make-up artist in my early twenties and worked for a professional dowser/photographer. It was fascinating to watch him use a pendulum to test film before a photo shoot. This man later told me that he believed I had some 'fairy blood,' which inspired me to further explore my psychic abilities.

"In my early thirties I had an unforgettable encounter with an intensely bright being of light that radically shifted my consciousness in the most wonderful of ways. For the next several years I attended Celtic and Egyptian meditations, which enhanced my intuition.

"I feel that magic in its many forms should only be used for self-transformation, healing, spiritual development, and divination. I am usually more accurate with a first reading over the telephone, especially when dealing with strong or powerful personalities.

"Most of my clients have told me that my readings have a grounding and healing effect. I am currently reading for a varied clientele which includes artists, musicians, financial analysts, designers, secretaries, and other tarot readers."

When asked to cite specific cases, she consulted her notes and related the following case studies with dates.

In 1994, Stephanie consulted Margaret, wanting to know what to expect from her move to Alaska. She was told that she would become involved in documentary films about Native

American tribes, which was confirmed a year later. Margaret also predicted during the reading that Stephanie would meet and fall in love with a handsome man who was part Alaskan Indian, which was confirmed six months later. However, Margaret then saw that they would be separated, which did not make sense as they were madly in love. Months later the man fell from a fishing boat and drowned. In 1996, while giving Stephanie another reading, Margaret felt a presence in the room and realized it was J., the deceased boyfriend. Margaret informed Stephanie that he was present; upon hearing this Stephanie asked her to state the color of the door of his house in Alaska; Margaret replied, "blue," which was correct. The deceased boyfriend asked Margaret to remind Stephanie that he had intended to marry her as he had told her. Stephanie confirmed this to Margaret as well.

In February 1996, P., an unemployed assistant clothing designer, wanted to know where her next job would be. Margaret predicted that her new job would begin in two weeks for a famous designer whose entire line that season was blue. P. telephoned to confirm this two weeks later.

In June 1996, N. asked Margaret during a reading if she should travel to Paris for her aunt's funeral, as the trip would cause severe financial problems for her. Margaret saw that she should go and predicted that she would discover a valuable antique in her aunt's apartment. N. returned two weeks later with the good news that Margaret's predictions had indeed been correct.

In July 1996, D., an assistant to a New York City private investigator, asked Margaret during a reading if she should gamble in Atlantic City that weekend. Margaret told her that she should, because she would win some money. D. later telephoned to confirm that she had won over four thousand dollars.

In January 1997, W., a beautiful fifty-year-old woman,

wanted to know if she would be alone for the rest of her life, as she had not met any men suitable for her in years. Margaret told W. that she would meet a wonderful Virgo man in several months and marry him approximately one year later. Margaret later heard that this indeed had come true for W. and that she was now married to the Virgo man.

In July 1997, Margaret predicted during a reading with a professional disc jockey that on the upcoming weekend he would meet a pretty blonde who was financially well off. He later telephoned to confirm that he had met and dated a pretty blond heiress.

O. was unemployed and overweight when she consulted Margaret in October 1997. During the reading, O. asked what type of low-impact exercise she should do to lose weight. Margaret told her that she already had the answer to her exercise problem in the back of one of her large closets and that it looked like a bicycle. O. telephoned the following day to report that in the back of the closet she had found a stationary exercise bicycle that had never been used.

Margaret predicted in January 1998, that F., a professional guitarist who wanted to know the future of a band he recently joined, would be discovered by another band while playing with the first one. She also told him that the present band would perform in nice clubs and that their agent would get the big record companies to see them, but that they would not be signed by any of the companies. Later that year, F. telephoned Margaret to tell her that the predictions had indeed been accurate, and that he was contacted by another band. They had seen his performance, and their style of music was more compatible with his.

In May 1998, T. asked during a reading if the man she had fallen in love with would ever commit to marriage. Margaret predicted their engagement by January 1999, and that they would be married the following summer. T. later called to confirm that they were engaged in December 1998, and planned to marry in the summer of 1999.

C., a financial analyst, consulted Margaret in September 1998, to see if there was a better paying job in his future. She predicted that at the end of the year a job paying three times more would come his way. He telephoned to confirm the prediction one month later.

In December 1998, V. consulted Margaret wanting to know if there were any problems with the house she had just purchased, even though it had passed inspections. She predicted that it shouldn't have passed the inspections because there were structural weaknesses and other problems with the house. Unfortunately, V. called several months later to confirm Margaret's predictions.

Judging from the amazing case histories that have been related to me, Margaret's predictions have a very high rate of accuracy. It is clear that she was born to do this work, and it is her true calling.

Fahrusha (Rosanne Shaffer)
Tel.: 212-254-5948
      212-529-4775

Fahrusha, an oriental dancer and actress for many years, adopted her stage name for her professional psychic career as well. Not only a gifted tarot-card reader, she is equally adept in palmistry, interpreting handwriting, and reading tea leaves. In addition, Fahrusha is also an expert at reading photographs, and she can successfully map out character, motivations, health problems, and so on from snapshots.

Fahrusha has traveled the world, actively seeking places

where she can absorb energy, such as stone circles, pyramids, and other ancient monuments. She believes the ancients situated their monuments with sacred geometry and powerful earth energy in mind.

Fahrusha also has a psychic resonance with animals, especially cats. She has read for many people who have cats as pets and is able to detect their animals' emotions and ailments simply by stroking them; the pets usually come to Fahrusha instinctively.

Fahrusha provided me with the following anecdotes:

One day, at the Superior Copy Shop in New York City, Fahrusha and Alan Gershwin, the son of George Gershwin and a famous songwriter in his own right, paused to chat. With no previous knowledge of his life, Fahrusha correctly identified his son's name as Adrian.

One night Fahrusha had a dream about a neighbor named Nina who had two little boys. In the dream, a voice told her that Nina would have a third child, a girl. She mentioned the dream to her friend; a year later Nina had a little girl.

Lisa, a New York department store executive, consulted Fahrusha concerning her desire to have another child, although her physician doubted it would happen. Fahrusha told her she would be pregnant within three months. In spite of the doctor's doubts, the woman indeed became pregnant as Fahrusha predicted.

Marian, an executive from New Jersey, consulted Fahrusha about her career and was told that she would leave the country due to an irresistible offer from a foreign institution. She replied that she wouldn't consider leaving the United States. She is now working in Great Britain.

Ravi, a computer professional, had been told by several astrologers that he would marry Miss V., a student with whom he was in love. Fahrusha disagreed with the other predictions, saying that the relationship would end unhappily. He would, she said, meet a small woman with glasses within a year who would return his affections. He left the reading distressed and disbelieving. He returned over a year later to tell Fahrusha that all had happened as she had predicted.

Hired to read cards at a party near Stamford, Connecticut, Fahrusha agreed to give the hostess a reading before the event began. As soon as the woman sat down for the reading, Fahrusha queried, "Are you pregnant?" Fahrusha said this in wonderment, as the woman had four children and a career. Mrs. McC. replied cautiously, "Well...it is possible." Fahrusha commented, "Pregnancy is so strong around you that I wouldn't be surprised if it were twins." Both women laughed. Several months later, Fahrusha telephoned her hoping to get a recommendation for another house party. The housekeeper answered the telephone, saying that Mrs. McC. was resting in bed, not to be disturbed. Alarmed, Fahrusha inquired about her health. The housekeeper replied, "Oh no, she's fine. Haven't you heard? She's having triplets."

Recently, Fahrusha broke one of her rules by telephoning a client. (She generally does not initiate contact with clients, except to return their calls.) She had an urgent dream concerning a regular, Stacy, an airline attendant. In the dream she heard Stacy call for help, very perturbed. She telephoned Stacy later to see if she was okay. Stacy later returned the call to say that the very night Fahrusha had dreamed about her, Stacy was on a particularly harrowing flight over the Atlantic, culminating in her being fired from her job. She became very upset over this and had planned to call the psychic for help.

In addition to her popularity with people in the entertainment business, Fahrusha has many corporate and professional clients. She is very intuitive and has often been consulted by other psychics. Combining her genuine psychic talent with entertainment, she has developed into a very popular and professional reader.

Herald, Joy
434 Caldwell Drive
Wyckoff, NJ 07481
Tel.: 201-652-1177
    201-625-0365

Joy Herald, described as an international psychic medium, became aware of her abilities while attending college, eventually giving up her corporate career to become a full-time psychic. Joy went on to study with various professionals in the field.

Joy gave her first prediction to an older gentleman who had come for a consultation. While reading his cards, she "saw" a wedding in progress; however, she thought this unlikely because of her client's age. She went ahead and gave the prediction because she had been taught to follow her psychic instincts instead of common sense. Much to hers and her client's surprise, the event indeed took place later that month.

Joy felt compelled to tell a woman during a reading to buy an amethyst ring. The woman was puzzled. Why? Joy had no idea, but her guides told her that this would be important in the woman's life, and would be connected to someone she would meet. The woman followed the advice, and on the first opportunity went to a store with the intent to purchase the ring. The salesman was very pleasant and helpful, and a friendship developed between them. A year later the woman and the salesman married, all because of Joy's advice.

Emma L. was told during a reading that she had a liver problem and should seek medical advice. The doctor confirmed Joy's psychic insight.

In a missing-persons case, Joy did a reading for Mrs. V., touching only garments worn by her missing daughter. Joy informed the client that her daughter had gone off with an older man who spoke a different language, but that Mrs. V. would be contacted by the daughter at a later date. This all turned out as Joy had predicted.

Today Joy teaches and lectures on various psychic subjects in addition to her private and business readings.

Hoffman, Judy
165 East 89th Street
New York, NY 10128
Tel.: 212-534-6279

Judy Hoffman is a young woman from Pittsburgh, Pennsylvania, where she attended Carnegie Mellon University, receiving a bachelor's degree in both theater and writing—not the typical description for a psychic and tarot reader.

She began her professional career as an actress, acting teacher, and writer, and, much to her surprise, eventually settled into that of tarot reader after having a lot of success at it.

Judy uses ordinary playing cards in her readings instead of the customary tarot decks. She reads in layouts of three times seven cards, one each for the past, the immediate future, and the long-term future. I heard of Judy from my close friend, the actress Tina Louise, for whom she gave a very accurate reading.

In one of her predictions for a client who was a Florida hotel executive, she gave the exact date when her divorce would occur, as well as describing her next husband, even giving the exact date of his marriage proposal!

During another consultation, she told a college girl, Patti H., that she would meet a man named Mike during some type of exercise activity and that he would wear a uniform. Sometime later the girl did meet a fellow named Mike, a marine, while swimming.

Among many predictions she has given me, on June 11, 1993, she told me that I would be involved in "a dispute over work or money with a woman initialed S." In January 1994 I settled a dispute over work done for my son-in-law, and received his money from a woman with the initial S. She also accurately predicted that I would be offered an interview by CNN; which I was (though it was ultimately canceled due to the California fires).

For another client, a housewife at the time, Judy predicted the creation, publication, and phenomenal success of a bestselling self-help book. At the time the future author had no idea of the meaning of the prediction.

Judy told a client, who had never married, that she would meet her future husband through her brother. The client scoffed at the idea, saying that her brother lived out of state and had no intention of introducing her to anyone. Within six months of a visit to her brother, she met a man who became her husband. It turned out that the brother had already introduced them several years before, but there had been no attraction then.

Judy also accurately predicted a scandalous affair between two married television executives. She forecast that the scandal would pass and they would end up together. They are getting married this year.

She told a British filmmaker that she would win an award—the woman won first place in her category—and this was her first attempt at filmmaking.

Judy told a well-known musician he would be nominated for a Grammy Award, but that he would not win.

She predicted the planning, building, and funding of a condominium cruise ship, the first of its kind. At the time of the reading the client had major fears that the investors for the project would back out. The ship is now selling the condo units and is set to launch next year.

Judy recently faxed me a dream that she had at 12:05 A.M. on December 4, 1995. The dream concerned an earthquake that she thought would happen in Bogota, Colombia. The events of the dream are detailed as follows.

"In the dream, I am just waking up from *having* a dream. It is morning and I am recalling the dream. I realize the dream I had within the dream was about a massive earthquake in Bogota, Colombia, during which I witnessed incredible destruction. I see two men on the highest floor of a damaged high-rise building. They are part of a rescue team and they are surveying the damage. I decide to telephone Dr. Holzer to report this dream. I make the call and have a brief conversation where I retell this dream...."

Retelling of the dream as she reported to me: "I am in Bogota, Colombia, in a high-rise apartment building I look out the window and other buildings are shaking. They explode and crumble. This goes on for about three minutes. Then a few men, maybe inspectors, come into my apartment. They say the earthquake was 7.5 on the Richter scale. (I wake up at 5 A.M. I go back to sleep from 6 to 9 A.M. and dream a second dream.)"

Retelling of the second dream: "I am at Hans Holzer's desk reporting the earlier dream. I say 'It will be a 7.5, thousands of people, some of them wealthy and prominent, will die. It will happen between 8 A.M. and 1 P.M. People should get out if they can and they shouldn't go if they don't have to."

Unfortunately, the accuracy of this dream was revealed three years later. On January 27, 1999, in Colombia, in the same province as Bogota, a major earthquake occurred killing many, many people.

Hughes, Irene
500 N. Michigan, Suite 1040
Chicago, IL 60611
Tel.: 312-467-1140

Irene Hughes is the premier psychic of the Midwest. I have known her for years. She has two careers, one as a psychic reader and the other as an astrologer. Even though she tries to keep the two separate, clients may contact her for both services.

Ms. Hughes has had the gift of "second sight" from early childhood. Born in the south, and of Scottish–Native American heritage, she practiced as a trance medium for several years but later decided to concentrate on spiritual counseling and claims to use spirit communication to aid her. Reportedly, she is controlled by a "spirit teacher" and will not divulge his name. Her consultations and counseling sessions are thirty minutes long. Generally, she covers both personal and professional situations for her clients, sometimes involving herself in medical projects and healing as well.

On occasion Ms. Hughes has worked with medical doctors, without ever meeting or seeing the patient for whom she gives a diagnosis. All this is done through mail; at present she does not administer healing in person.

In 1967 she received a suggestion to become an astrologer, which she rejected. Eventually she reconsidered and studied with Norman Aarons, which enabled her to teach astrology for three semesters at a community college. Studying astrology and interpreting charts helped her to better understand herself and others, she says. In interpreting clients' charts, she prefers to adhere to strictly astrological concepts. "However, if something is revealed to me psychically, I then say 'this is a psychic impression above and beyond the mathematical calculations in your chart,' for I feel that being a psychic helps me to see different meanings more deeply."

Irene Hughes is one of the few reputable psychics who gives readings by mail because she is skillful in psychometry. Psychometry is how she solves police cases. For instance, she is given an object of a murdered individual from which she tries to receive an impression of the crime.

She accompanied me on ghost hunts long before Brad Steiger decided to do the same with her and record his impressions in the book *Irene Hughes on Psychic Safari*. Ms. Hughes has also written a book called *ESPecially Irene*.

The list of Ms. Hughes's public predictions, especially concerning public figures is impressive—especially the ones that turned out to be true. She predicted Vice President Spiro Agnew's downfall, due to legal problems; she has a Chicago talk-show host as witness. Ms. Hughes accurately predicted the assassination of both John and Robert Kennedy, the remarriage of Jacqueline Kennedy, and the 1967 war in the Middle East.

Ms. Hughes does accept new clients for both psychic and astrology consultations. However, those wishing for personal interviews may have a several-month wait for an appointment as she is very busy. Her office is staffed by two full-time assistants and a secretary. Ms. Hughes also writes a syndicated newspaper column and is planning to write more books about her work.

Jaegers, Beverly
The U.S. Psi Squad
P.O. Box 29396
St. Louis, MO 63126

I met Mrs. Jaegers many years ago on a talk show in St. Louis, Missouri, where she still resides. In the 1970s, Beverly Jaegers became justly known as an accurate psychic who helped police solve crime cases. As a result, she formed a group originally called the Psychic Rescue Squad. For eleven years, Mrs. Jaegers and her squad of helpers have actively been involved in over one hundred cases, fighting crime through ESP; her group later included both former and active police officers. Beverly Jaegers, a no-nonsense person with six children, is not exactly Madame Arcati of *Blithe Spirit*.

When trying to engage Mrs. Jaegers in missing persons cases, she would expect to hear not only all details of the disappearance, but also to touch a garment or other object the missing person would have touched—preferably something that would have been used near the time of the disappearance.

Mrs. Jaegers also works well in unsolved murder cases, but that usually requires her visiting the place where the body was found. Her reputation is such that police departments gladly cooperate with her.

Today Mrs. Jaegers trains people in ESP development and also offers correspondence courses related to her gifts and work. Mrs. Jaegers is not exactly publicity-shy, but then she does have some remarkable evidence of her success. Missing persons and crime and detective work in general are her forte.

Joyce, Elizabeth
P.O. Box 99
Chalfont, PA 18914
Tel.: 215-996-0646
    212-877-0717

I have known Elizabeth Joyce for several years and have a complete record of her predictions and prophecies. Miss Joyce's services range from simple private sessions to giving lectures, seminars, radio appearances, writing books and much more. Originally Miss Joyce gained fame as a model, discovering her psychic gifts later, which are truly spectacular at times.

On July 15, 1993, she sent me the following written statement, "Giordano will be the next Mayor of New York City and a woman will be governor of New Jersey." Well, Giuliani is close enough and we all know about Christine Whitman, who became governor in 1993.

In September 1997 she made the following prediction to *Fate* magazine about the presidential family. "A dark-haired woman named Veronica will upset the Clinton Administration in early 1998, and Clinton may not deliver the State of the Union Address. An angry blonde will bring forth the truth, this will be verified by others later, and Clinton will be impeached late in that year." "Veronica" is of course Monica, again proof that many psychic impressions are auditory rather than visual for clairvoyants. Linda Tripp naturally is the "angry blonde."

Elizabeth Joyce has a genuine psychic gift.

Karter, Kathleen
66 West 94th Street
New York, NY 10025
Tel.: 212-663-7434

Kathleen Karter is truly one of a handful of great mediums in the United States. She is a gifted psychic reader, competent trance medium, and Spiritualist.

I first met Mrs. Karter in 1975 and have kept in contact with her since for occasional readings and in order to test her considerable skills. In some cases I have been called to accompany her in sessions to resolve a psychic problem in which she served as the medium.

During our first meeting, when she did not know anything about me, she stated that my marriage would be over by 1980 (it was); that I would travel to the West Coast for professional reasons in connection with films that had something to do with apparitions (I did, as I wrote and produced some of the *In Search Of* segments of the series in 1977); and that I would begin a society or foundation (I started the New York Committee for the Investigation of Paranormal Occurrences two years later).

In November 1975, she read for me again and gave the following prediction: She said that I would cross the water in connection with an old house, and she heard German spoken; there was negotiating going on for money, and books and "things" would be moving in Europe, in 1976. Well, about three weeks later I received an unexpected offer for the house I owned in Austria and needed to fly there immediately. I sold the house after considerable negotiations; books and "things" were indeed moved out of the house and left in Europe for me.

To be sure there are many things she predicted that have not occurred, at least not yet, and many never can because she imposed time limits in her readings. But the fact that she was able to accurately predict things that did occur in such great detail is astonishing and convinced me of her gifts.

Levy, Elizabeth A.
175 West 13th Street
New York, NY 10011
Tel.: 212-243-0579

Elizabeth Levy is an ordained minister. I interviewed her, and when I asked her to relate some of her predictions, she told me the following.

"In the early part of January 1999, I predicted that if my client called her uncle and asked him to lend her the money, not only would he be nice and gracious, he would definitely come through with the money. My client just called me earlier this week to inform me that she did speak with her uncle and he did lend her the money and was very cordial. I had also told her that she would not need to declare bankruptcy, and that people would help her. Indeed they have. Previously I told this client (in 1996) that she would have marital difficulties, but would not divorce her husband, even though she might come close to leaving him. It is now 1999, and although they still have some problems, they are very much together."

She also cited that "a woman who lives and conducts her private practice in New England as a healer would marry the man she was dating and that they were a good match. I made this prediction both to her and her sister in 1997. The woman's sister informed me that my client did marry this man in the fall of 1998."

McAlester, Colette
Tel.: 972-702-9442

Colette McAlester, who was born in Paris and is bilingual, has been doing her work as a psychic rather quietly from her Dallas, Texas, base. Colette gave me a telephone reading which I found to be impressive and accurate.

Other accurate readings include one for a client who works in television. She revealed that "someone connected with the show *Walker, Texas Ranger* would die." In January one of the stuntmen appearing on the show suffered a fatal heart attack on the set.

L.I., a regular client, was told that she would receive a promotion with a raise in August. This was eighteen months ago. L.I. disagreed, as raises were only given in January at her place of work. Nevertheless, the following August she unexpectedly received a raise, with another following in January!

In another prediction, Colette told her client, who was worried about losing her job, that she would not be fired, but her boss would be. And so it came to pass.

Colette has a following of clients from all over the world and, in addition to her psychic gift is a professional astrologer.

Moreno, Maria
2045 Casa Linda Drive
West Covino, CA 91791
Tel.: 818-966-7500

I first heard of a "fabulous Mexican psychic" named Maria Moreno from a fellow author and researcher, Jess Stearn, who had tested Maria and found her extremely gifted.

I went to see Maria in June of 1981, and at that time I am sure she did not know anything about me, as I simply said that I had heard of her from friends.

In this first session she began by going into a trance and letting her "control" speak through her. Even though her English wasn't good, we understood each other. She mentioned Dino DeLaurentiis, and at that time Dino had nothing to do with me or my work; that came several years later. She mentioned the name Rosemary, whom I only met three years later; we are still very close friends. She also mentioned that a "big politician, P., would be helpful." I met Senator Claiborne Pell several years later for the first time! Following these revelations came the most controversial part of the session. Suddenly Maria asked me whether I could place someone named Eileen in my life—a lady whom she felt was very important and with whom I had worked. She also mentioned a man named John, whom I had met through Eileen, both of whom had long since passed over. I immediately recognized them to be the late Eileen Garrett and the writer John Latouche—how could Maria have known this?

Quickly I looked around her modest apartment while she stepped away for a moment, wondering if I would find some of my books in which these two people were mentioned. I found none. Frankly, Maria's English at that time was such that I doubt she could have read and understood such books.

I saw Maria again on June 15, 1987; a very hot afternoon in Hollywood. Actually, she expected a Mr. Wood, as I had decided not to use my real name so that she would not be able to do any research. It made no difference. Her "control," whom she simply called "the hunchback," took over and greeted me like an old friend. I also noticed that the trance "control" spoke excellent English, while Maria in her normal condition did not. This second reading was even more interesting than the first six years earlier. Contracts, deals, and again, Dino DeLaurentiis were mentioned. By now I had already met DeLaurentiis and encountered contractual difficulties with him. Someone named James wanted to be acknowledged from the other side, "like a preacher," she said. I was very close to the late Bishop James Pike, with whom I had made a film, and about whose death I had written a book. She also said that an institute would come about (it seems that nearly came about in 1994). The other matters were personal, but also very specific as to names, identities of the people she mentioned—but no specific time element, which did not surprise me as that aspect of readings is rarely accurate.

I also found it remarkable that the second reading duplicated much that had been stated in the first one, held six years earlier, even though she had not taken notes and probably would not have remembered.

Maria remains a qualified and gifted psychic with the ability to give names and specific circumstances.

Morton, Pat
2825 S. Edward's Drive
Nashville, TN 37211
Tel.: 615-833-7574

This Nashville seer of Irish, Scottish, and Native American background discovered her clairvoyant abilities as people came to her for counseling over the years.

Her many case histories also include the following anecdotes.

In 1989 she predicted that a dark-skinned Middle Eastern leader would cause problems, including what she called a "Saudi War," within two weeks—precisely the time when Saddam Hussein invaded Kuwait.

A Memphis client once asked Pat whether her daughter would win a certain beauty contest. Pat assured her only that a girl wearing a peach-colored dress would be the winner. It turned out that the dress her daughter wore was indeed peach and she won the contest.

Reading at a psychic fair, Pat saw a dark-haired young woman who inquired about her love life. Pat described a tall, handsome, dark-haired man, yet felt that this relationship was no longer in place. The woman acknowledged he had been her fiancé, but that they were no longer together. Toward the end of the reading Pat announced that the young woman would be getting a letter from her former fiancé. A strange expression crossed her face and she said coldly "I don't think so." Pat shrugged, and replied, "I see what I see—you'll get a letter from him very soon."

Later in the day the woman approached Pat once more and said, "You know, I have to tell you that the young man, my fiancé—we didn't get married because he was killed." Pat looked at her for a long moment and said "I can't help it. I see you getting a letter from him." A year later this same woman telephoned Pat's office to report a strange and wonderful outcome to that prediction. It seems that the young man's brother was cleaning out his home and came across a letter the man had written but never sent to his fiancé. The brother had forwarded it to the young woman, and the unlikely prediction of a letter from a dead man had come true.

Once Pat received a telephone call from a mother whose son had been found dead in his car. The police had ruled the death a suicide, but the mother was adamant that her son would not have committed suicide. He had recently graduated from school, and taken his "dream job" with a social services agency. After examining a photo of the young man, Pat told the mother that she felt the boy had been the victim of murder, and that the gun which was found on the backseat beside him was not the gun which fired the fatal bullet. She urged the mother to check with the sheriff's office to ensure ballistics tests had been run. In fact, they had not—the police had been convinced the death was a suicide, and so did not order the test. After further investigation, it was discovered that the bullet that took the boy's life was not fired from the gun found with his body. The cause of death was changed from suicide to murder, and the case was reopened. To date, this case has not been solved.

A couple came to see Pat just before they were to leave on a trip West. Pat predicted that they would arrive safely, both coming and going, but there would be mechanical problems with their transportation. That night Pat received a call from the couple letting her know they were safe. It seems that the private plane in which they took their trip needed to make an emergency landing. They both laughed, and said it was a great comfort to them, that Pat had assured them they would arrive safely!

In one reading, Pat predicted that a client would soon have another child. The mother of four laughed, saying that her husband had undergone a vasectomy to prevent such an occurrence. Within three months she was pregnant with her fifth child, a boy.

In 1993 Susan G. was taking a breather from having babies. She and her husband were planning to wait several years before deciding whether or not to have a third child. To that end, she had the Norplant birth-control device implanted after the birth of her daughter. She asked Pat whether she and her husband would have any more children. Pat's surprising answer was "I see you pregnant this year." "Oh no, that's impossible," Susan replied, "I'm on Norplant." Pat shrugged.

"Can't help what I see. This isn't a really good time for you to get pregnant, though; the best time would be sometime between your twenty-ninth and thirtieth birthdays."

Several months later, Susan became one of the .02 percent of women who get pregnant using Norplant. Unfortunately, it was a tubal pregnancy and she had to undergo surgery. As a result of this experience, she decided to have another child. She bore her second daughter, Gaylen, between her twenty-ninth and thirtieth birthdays. She recalls "Pat was right; it was the best time for me to get pregnant! After difficult pregnancies and deliveries with my first two children, Gaylen was a joy to carry and was born easily at home with my husband in attendance."

In the fall of 1998, Susan's middle child, Caitlin, had been ill for some time. Running a high fever and complaining of severe headaches, Caitlin had been in and out of the emergency room and various doctors' offices for over a week. They couldn't find anything wrong with her and even ordered a CAT scan in the hopes of pinpointing the problem, all to no avail. Finally, at the end of her rope, she telephoned Pat, who felt that it was an ear infection and told Susan to have the doctor look at the area once more. Susan made another appointment with the exasperated physician for Monday morning. Over that weekend, the infection came to a head and was highly visible when they finally made it to the doctor's office, much to the pediatrician's surprise!

A distraught mother went to see Pat in the spring of 1997, searching for her teenage daughter. She had last been seen in the company of a family acquaintance: a man who was known to have a criminal record involving minors. This man had also vanished. The police and family feared that the girl had been abducted. Pat felt that the girl had left voluntarily and would be spotted in November in the Tampa, Florida, area still in the company of the older man, but they would be apprehended in Texas, not Florida. In fact, the girl and man were seen in the Tampa Bay area in November and were later picked up by police across the Texas state line. The girl had indeed left on her own.

In 1993, a client was concerned about her husband's prospects for future employment. Pat told her that he would receive an offer from a company in or around Atlanta, Georgia, they would relocated, and that within five years the company would offer him a partnership. Oddly enough, she also predicted a second company offering him a chance to relocate to Europe, with an increase in salary, at the same time he was offered the partnership! In April 1978, nearly five years from the date of the original prediction, the client called Pat to inform her that they had relocated to Atlanta, and her husband had been offered both the partnership *and* the European job offer.

Pat Morton presently works with police and business professionals as well as giving private readings.

O'Dell, Allison
P.O. Box 144
New York, NY 10012
Tel.: 212-886-4814

Allison O'Dell has a cable television show called *Atlantean Tarot With Allison* in the New York City area. Miss O'Dell bases her tarot readings largely on the philosophy of Edgar Cayce. She gives both tarot card readings and astrological readings, including elements of numerology.

Miss O'Dell states that her purpose is to bring clients "to a higher level of consciousness."

I interviewed Miss O'Dell recently and she noted the following predictions.

"I remember having a client who was very concerned

about his living arrangements. He had just broken up with his girlfriend and she lived in the same neighborhood. He had an idea to purchase an apartment in a different neighborhood. I cautioned him against it, as it appeared in the cards that his whole life would be thrown into upheaval if he moved. Several weeks later he telephoned to tell me that his offices for work had been moved to the very same block on which he lived, so it became very convenient for him to stay in the old place!

"I read for a client once who had recently split with a boyfriend of several years. She was asking me questions about possibilities of relationships with certain other men. Everything kept turning up negatively in the cards, and I advised her against becoming involved with any of the men she had asked about. Eventually, I noticed that the cards were pointing to an old relationship reentering her life, and I got a very strong sense that she would be married very soon. She was incredulous and couldn't make any sense of it. About one month later she telephoned to inform me that, in fact, her old boyfriend had made contact with her again and had asked her to marry him! They were married within six months of the reading.

"A while back I did a reading for a client who was having some difficulty at work. He felt he should be paid more for his efforts with the company. I saw the turmoil in his office, and didn't really see the bosses budging on a salary increase for him. However, I could sense very strongly that there would soon be an influx of a great deal of money around him. He couldn't understand how I could see more money around him if I didn't believe it would be coming to him through his job. Several weeks later he telephoned to let me know that, in fact, he was not able to negotiate for a higher salary, but his uncle had died unexpectedly and left his fortune to his nephews! It was complete windfall and a surprise, but we had seen it in the cards.

"I did a reading for a friend who had recently broken up with a boyfriend of several years and was very distraught over it but knew it was the right thing to do. She had also been frustrated with her work as a musician, as it had been on hold for a while. I got an extremely positive sense from the reading, and could see that within one year, she would be romantically involved with a new individual whom I sensed would be a Capricorn, and he would be able to help her with her musical career. I also sensed a Virgo male who would be helpful to her. She telephoned about a year later to tell me that she had met a Capricorn male and that they had moved in together. Additionally, he was a musician as well and had helped her to start a new band and begin production work for her new music. They are also being helped by their new manager, a Virgo male!

"Recently I did a short reading for a woman who was having trouble at her place of work. She had only been with her new firm for several months, but there had been some modifications at the management level that made her uncomfortable, and she wasn't sure what to do. I assured her not to worry because she would soon be working at a different firm. She was incredulous because she really had just started working there and couldn't see herself making another big move. In addition, I predicted this would be happening within two to three weeks, and during this time I saw her also initiating a new, very committed love relationship. This truly surprised her, because she had been very focused on work lately and wasn't even interested in finding out about relationships. She had also not been involved with anyone for over a year and found it difficult to believe that everything would change so soon. Two weeks later she called to tell me that she couldn't believe it herself, but she had received an offer from another firm and would be starting the new job immediately; and also she had met someone new, just as the cards had predicted, but she wasn't sure yet if this would in fact turn into a serious relationship, as we had 'seen.' However, she called about a month later to inform me that they were beginning to discuss marriage!"

Eloquent and serious about her work, Miss O'Dell delivers some surprisingly accurate information during her readings.

Palmer, Salina
15353 Weddington
Sherman Oaks, CA 91411
Tel.: 818-906-9857

Salina Palmer is the daughter of famed English astrologer Ernest Palmer, who was also a well-known writer. (Incidentally, Miss Palmer was born on a flight bringing her parents to the United States.) Living in the Hollywood vicinity, it was only a matter of time before she became known as "psychic to the stars," as well as the in-house psychic for Paramount Studios.

Some of her noted claims included the late Jim Morrison, the lead singer of the Doors. Among other things, she told him she saw a headstone in Paris with the date 1971. Unfortunately, this did come true—he died in 1971—and as a result of her prediction Salina did not want to give any more readings for a while.

Ava Gabor, the celebrated actress, was a friend of Salina's father. Once Salina gave her a reading in which she described a scene in television involving grass and a pitchfork and predicted Ms. Gabor would be very successful in television at a time when that seemed very unlikely. The television show turned out to be *Green Acres,* which ran for years and made Ms. Gabor a television star.

Even though Salina Parker is sought after by many people in the entertainment field, she does give readings for those not of celebrity status. Lately, Salina has discovered she also has the power of healing and is exploring this newfound gift.

Papapetros, Maria
140 East 55th Street
New York, NY 10021
Tel.: 212-935-4441

Maria Papapetros has been giving readings to her faithful clients in both Los Angeles and New York for many years.

I met Maria for the first time in Los Angeles on March 30, 1990, and at that time I felt her work was more about spiritual counseling than about predictions. However, one prediction she made for me came true eight years later.

A gentleman from Kentucky had a reading with Maria in 1997. The man's son, John, had left home to join a religious sect, and he needed counseling concerning this situation. Maria's advice was to write a letter to John every day. In these letters the father was to tell John of his unconditional love and that there would always be a warm and loving welcome there for him. The father was instructed not to mail these letters, but to keep them for thirty days, and at the end of the month to destroy them. John would be able to pick up the loving vibrations from the letters his father wrote to him. The father followed Maria's instructions, and fifteen days later John returned home.

In a reading for the famed singer and actress Vanessa Williams, Maria kept receiving the word Disney. Vanessa was chosen to sing the theme song for the Disney animated film *Pocahontas*.

Maria gave Dianne a reading in March 1997. Maria told her she would meet a Middle Eastern or West Asian man. He would be in New York on business and they would meet briefly on his last day in the United States, but they would keep in touch. She also told Dianne that she would soon be working with computers doing something internationally. Dianne, at this point in her life, did not even know how to turn on a computer. The man Maria predicted materialized in the form of an Indian gentleman, who was indeed on the last day of his trip. They have remained in contact and he has asked her to take up the computer to enable her to help with his international networking.

Maria has developed a very good reputation among both her famous and nonfamous clientele.

Paretti, Catherine
400 East 70th Street
New York, NY 10021
Tel.: 212-472-3251

Catherine is both a psychic and healer. She became a healer as a result of curing her own severe illness. For eight years, Catherine was bound to a wheelchair, but her determination and efforts at self-healing eventually cured her. In 1975 she had a near-death experience and in 1982 she was struck by a nerve disorder. She overcame all of these hardships to become a successful practicing psychic and healer.

In 1987 I began to help Catherine in her psychic development and saw her weekly in order to test her abilities. Numerous readings contained situations and data which later proved correct.

A remarkable example of Catherine's predictive abilities include one instance in which she stated during a session on June 17, 1987, that there would be "a breakthrough...two men clasping hands with joy...movies...entry...very good movie and money." In 1988 I met my partner for films in Europe; the first film was in fact called *The Entry*. Her prediction had in fact come true.

A client of Catherine Paretti's named Gabrielle V. related the following story: "I consider this to be Catherine's most exciting and accurate prediction of world events. In August preceding the February World Trade Center bombing, Catherine suddenly had a flash of this tragedy. 'Downtown is not safe this winter,' she said. I commented, 'Catherine, downtown is a pretty big place, *where* downtown? And why should I avoid it anyhow?' She went on to tell me that 'it' was going to be near the bridges, perhaps the Twin Towers. She saw a giant explosion, downtown was sealed off, people weren't expecting it. She saw the snow. It was not, she believed, a disaster having to do with carelessness or fuel sources like natural gas, but a deliberate horror, something to do with the Middle East. She was chillingly right."

In another instance the same client related, "I was initially flat-out rejected by my college of choice. Catherine, who has never had the opportunity to attend college and is unfamiliar with the admissions process, was unshakable in her belief that this indeed was the school I was going to attend. I put my faith in other institutions, but she asked me simply to call the school and try to speak to someone. I did manage to speak to a person who gave me an interview and took my application and essay in hand on the strength that a mistake may have been made. The admissions board reversed its decision swiftly and very easily. I was accepted within three weeks of the first letter.

"Catherine has not only predicted what jobs I would get during two of my exhaustive searches, but also when I would get them. Timing is notoriously difficult in the world of clairvoyance. Her advice, consisting of common sense, and her gift, has benefited me greatly in terms of understanding coworkers, timing, and presentation of my projects and proposals."

This client concluded by saying, "Catherine made predictions about the man I was going to marry for years. I became tired of hearing her go on about him. Just when I stopped believing her altogether (usually a foolhardy thing to do, I have found) the man I am going to marry this October stepped quietly into my life—exactly as she said and precisely as she described him."

Catherine Paretti is an extraordinary woman who, through her own diligence, cured herself and subsequently developed her gifts to help others.

Parker, Stephen T.
103 Winchester Street
Keene, NH 03431
Tel.: 603-358-3055

Stephen Parker is a talented screenwriter who also has a strong psychic ability. Mr. Parker gives readings in the New England area. During a recent conversation, I asked Mr. Parker to relate some of his most remarkable cases, including their resolutions. Here is what he said:

"A young female client who came to me for a tarot card reading had been through two traumatic losses of infant daughters. The first loss was the result of negligent monitoring and diagnosis of a pregnancy, resulting in a horrendous miscarriage during which the woman herself almost died. The second death involved an internally malformed infant daughter who died one week after birth. I predicted that she would become pregnant a third and fourth time and would deliver healthy girls, which did happen and can be verified by the client.

"In another instance, I received a frantic call from California regarding a thirteen-year-old boy who had wandered off around the Sunset Strip area of Hollywood and failed to rendezvous with his mother, who had brought him from England for the purposes of getting him psychic help (the boy had suffered a viral infection, which had resulted in mild brain damage two years prior). I psychically 'saw' him with a couple around ten years older than he was and felt that he was in danger if he stayed with them. I felt that the couple was trying to lure him away for sexual purposes. I also 'saw' that he initially had approached the couple, and so I asked his mother if he was prone to spontaneous outbursts of dialogue with complete strangers. She confirmed this behavior as being true. I told the boy's mother that I felt he would be returned unharmed. I prayed for this after speaking with her over the phone. The boy was located by police and returned safely after twenty-four hours."

Peters, Soni L.
P.O. Box 122
Buena Vista, PA 15018
Tel.: 412-751-5915
        412-751-7479

Soni Peters is largely a corporate consultant, but she will give private client readings. Ms. Peters has a high record of accuracy regarding her predictions.

In December 1994 she predicted a major job for a woman who did not do anything at the time and was, in fact, on Welfare. Soni "saw" the woman doing police work. In January 1995 she obtained a job as a corrections officer at a local jail.

Once, a woman consulted Ms. Peters because she had been told that she would not be able to have children. Contrary to this, Soni predicted she would have a baby, and the woman gave birth on January 2, 1999.

Another client consulted Soni in July 1993 and was told she would meet a man named Joe and fall in love with him. She really did meet such a man several weeks later, and they were married January 2, 1994.

Pignatelli, Anni
2017 Louella
Venice, CA 90291
Tel.: 310-391-3900

I met Ms. Pignatelli in 1979 and have consulted her concerning my work and personal life ever since, especially when I am in the Los Angeles area.

In 1980 Anni predicted that I would attend a wedding, but not in Los Angeles, and the woman would be older than the man. This did occur, but years later. Some of Anni's other predictions follow.

When one of her clients, an actress, went to see her, she described the man the actress would fall in love with, but Anni counseled against the marriage. The client did not heed the advice and the marriage ended in divorce. Anni also predicted that the client would be involved in a Jack Nicholson film, which also came to pass.

On July 6, 1994, Anni gave a reading for J. in which she "saw" the death of a young man with dark hair, someone J. was close to; she also "saw" the death of a woman a few years older than the man, and the two were together at the time. Anni predicted that a "dark" man was involved in it. On June 15, several weeks later, Ronald Goldman, the client's friend, was murdered along with Nicole Brown Simpson, and O. J. Simpson was the prime suspect.

Another client whom Anni saw in the summer of 1998 was told there was a huge problem with her boyfriend and a new person she had begun to see. This would happen when both would be in the client's home. The client thought this entirely unlikely. But in August her boyfriend stopped at her house unexpectedly while she was away. At that moment her telephone rang, and the new man she had started seeing left a message on the answering machine, which her boyfriend could hear. Needless to say he was not pleased.

Popper, Lyn
Tel.: 212-332-9913

Lyn has been a professional psychic for fifteen years. A native of Australia, she is extraordinarily gifted, running the gamut from going into full trances to using tarot cards as her "medium."

When Lyn gave me a reading, it proved to be extremely evidential, detailed, and contained names, places, and situations that I could relate to.

When asked about some of her cases, she related the following to me.

"Miss A. was an unknown costume designer who worked in Australia. I predicted her profession and that she would win an Oscar at the Academy Awards within two years. Much to her surprise she won an Academy Award within two years."

She also predicted that Mr. B., who was working as a waiter in New York City, would hear from an old friend within three days who would offer him a job in the film industry. This did happen within three days.

"Miss C. was living in Paris when she had her reading. I predicted that she would be living in New York within four years and that she would write a book about psychics. Four years later she wrote a book about psychics and was living in New York."

"Miss D. was not in a relationship when I gave her a reading. I predicted that she would marry the man of her dreams within three years and I mentioned the word green. She married a Mr. Green within three years."

In another instance, "Miss E. was working at an Australian television station. I predicted that a man with a beard named John would seek her out after one glance and that they would be together. A few months later a bearded man named John was in her office for a meeting. He happened to notice her working at her desk. When his meeting was finished she was gone for the day. He asked a coworker for her number, and subsequently they went out for dinner that night. They are now married."

During a reading for Miss F., who had not been in a relationship for quite some time since her husband had left, Lyn predicted that she would meet a man named Josef within a month's time; the client met Josef only three weeks later!

When Miss G. went to see Lyn, she had plans to travel overseas with a friend. During the reading Lyn predicted that Miss G. would be traveling overseas alone, and told her that the friend would not go with her. Three weeks later the client telephoned Lyn to say that the friend had passed away and she had traveled alone. Lyn also predicted a year later that the woman would return overseas and would ultimately work in London and Paris. Some time later Miss G. was offered a job in which she would live and work in London and Paris.

On another occasion Lyn told the following: "When Mrs. H. saw me she was not married. I predicted that she would marry a man with the initials A.T. and that his brothers would also have the initials A.T. Nine months later she married a man with the initials A.T., and his brothers also had the same initials. On her wedding day I predicted that she would have a baby boy, and I told her the month in which she would give birth. Mrs. H. had been told by medical doctors that she was unable to have children. She later gave birth to the baby boy in the predicted month."

During a reading Lyn told Miss I. that she would marry her soul mate. She predicted that they would be extremely happy together and that when their time came, they would die together. Miss I.'s friend sometime later telephoned Lyn to mention that Miss I. did indeed marry her soul mate and that they were both killed in a car accident returning from their honeymoon.

Mrs. J. was told during a reading that her husband would be offered a job that he could not refuse, but it would not be in New York. The client mentioned that she was looking to buy an apartment in New York. Lyn told Mrs. J. that she would not buy the apartment but would have a wonderful home elsewhere. Lyn also mentioned that the client would soon be pregnant; however, the client related that she was not intending to get pregnant anytime soon. Three months later Mrs. J. telephoned Lyn to say that her husband had accepted a position out of town and that she was pregnant.

Many of Ms. Popper's clients have attested to the accuracy of her predictions, and I have found her accurate in my own readings with her.

Rivera, Lucy
Tel.: 718-848-6302

Lucy Rivera has given psychic readings with considerable success for years and has developed a good following in the New York area, even though her main concern centers around her professional business career.

I met Ms. Rivera for the first time on July 15, 1984, and have seen her sporadically ever since. When Lucy has a strong psychic impression she immediately telephones me, especially when it concerns danger or matters of national interest. Due to my personal connections, I have always been able to forward her warnings or visions to the authorities without prejudice or, of course, guarantees.

Lucy visited me in January 1991, very concerned about a recurring vision which she had begun to have the previous year. In the vision she "saw" four airplanes over Manhattan, which she felt were threatening, and connected this to the then-ongoing struggle with Saddam Hussein. However, she also "saw" a bomb exploding in the Wall Street area of Manhattan with smoke rising, and described the people involved as dark skinned, wearing blue uniforms such as overalls, and people were running all over in great turmoil. She also felt that those who had caused this were from the Newark, New Jersey, area. She had the same basic vision again on January 15, 1991, and then she decided to see me about it so that I could warn authorities, which I did. When these events failed to materialize during the Persian Gulf War, I thought no more about it, until the tragic bombing over two years later. The dark-skinned perpetrators, eventually tried and found guilty, did indeed include some who were from New Jersey, and they wore overalls as they posed as repairmen when they parked the van containing the bomb.

Lucy resides in Brooklyn, New York, and does take appointments for private readings.

Roberta
Tel.: 718-459-4155

Roberta, who resides in the New York City area, has a large and devoted following because of the accuracy and reliability of her many predictions.

She has many astounding cases, including some of the following accounts, which she recently related to me.

S.T., a business executive, sent to see Roberta, and shortly into the reading Roberta "saw" the symbol of a black cloud with an airplane below it. This vision was followed by the number 8, the letters P, A, R, and then the numbers 7 and 4. She predicted an accident happening in the month of July. Roberta told her client "Don't fly from New York to Paris on a flight that starts with or adds up to the number 8." The client told her that she had just booked a TWA flight, number 800, New York to Paris, scheduled for July 17, 1996. Roberta immediately told her client to cancel her flight as Roberta "saw" a horrible crash. Roberta was so insistent that the client canceled the flight immediately. Less than two months later TWA Flight 800, New York to Paris, on July 17, 1996, crashed shortly after takeoff, with no survivors.

When K.S., a designer, went to Roberta, she told him of a dark-haired elderly woman standing behind him, who told Roberta her name was Pearl and that she was the man's grandmother. The client acknowledged that his grandmother's name was, in fact, Pearl. Roberta then went on to predict an accident which she hoped could be avoided. Roberta's vision included an airplane next to a demolished car with the letters CA and the number 8. She queried the client, asking if he would be traveling to California in the month of August. He answered yes. Roberta predicted that if he flew to California in August, his plane would not crash, but he would be involved in an automobile accident. The client told Roberta that it would be impossible to cancel the trip, but added that he would not rent a car as planned. The trip went without difficulties. However, on the last night, K.S.'s client became ill during dinner and asked if K.S. could drive him home in his car, only a fifteen-minute drive. K.S., remembering Roberta's prediction, thought it would be all right, since this was the last night and it was such a short ride. A few blocks from the restaurant they were involved in a terrible accident, but fortunately the air bags saved their lives.

Roberta gave a reading in December 1997 for A.J., a medical secretary. During the reading, she sensed a spirit around her client named Mary. The client confirmed that this was her mother, who had passed away over nineteen years ago. Roberta predicted that within a year, A.J. would meet someone named Robert whom she would like very much, and the man would have ties to Ireland, where A.J. had been born. She also said that next to the name Robert, she "saw" a castle with a shamrock next to it, and the man was somehow connected to castles. As expected, A.J. scheduled a reading for November 1998, almost a year later. The client told Roberta that she had indeed met a Robert, in whom she was very interested. She knew that this was the man Roberta had "seen" when he mentioned that as a child he used to spend his summer vacations at his aunt's house in Ireland where he played in an old deserted castle.

In October 1994, Roberta told L.C. that she sensed a dark-haired man around her with the name John. Her client said that John was her late father. Roberta then predicted that even though L.C. did not like her daughter's boyfriend, they would marry the following year and have a child. Roberta "saw" red roses next to two wedding rings and a silver baby rattle; but directly after that she "saw" black roses and two wedding rings to the left and the number 2. Roberta predicted this vision to mean that even though the daughter of the client would marry, there would be a divorce after the second anniversary. L.C. telephoned Roberta from England several years later and told me that the earlier events she had predicted unfolded exactly as Roberta had said.

J.C., an executive in the fashion industry, came to Roberta in July 1995. She was told that her husband Michael would be offered a new job within four months. Several months later the client's husband did receive such an offer. Roberta also told J.C. that there was a small blond woman named Betty near her. J.C. told the psychic that it was her late mother. Roberta also described the cemetery and the "gold cross" on the gravestone adjacent to her mother's. This was also confirmed later. Roberta read for J.C. again the following May and predicted that J.C. would change jobs within two years. J.C. had been at her present job for many years and was not considering a move in that she was happy. The prediction came true in December when she was offered a new job, which she took and loves.

Roberta has developed a large following of repeat clients

and accepts appointments for private readings in the Queens area of New York City where she resides and works.

Rogers, Rosanna
13214 Svec Avenue
Cleveland, OH 44120
Tel.: 216-751-1651

Rosanna Rogers has built a reputation on her ability to give
very precise and firm predictions for her clients. Rosanna
was born in Austria and spent
her formative years in Germany attending a convent high
school and college. She currently lives in a quiet neigh-
borhood of Cleveland where she has developed an international clientele.

Rosanna reads from a deck of cards that she developed
and bases her many predictions upon her interpretations of
the layouts. Some of her many case histories are detailed as
follows.

In the summer of 1987 a woman, whose husband was in
prison at the time, went to see Rosanna. The woman felt her
husband was falsely accused of the crime for which he was
incarcerated, but had no hope of his being exonerated, so she
decided to sell the apartment building they owned. But the
psychic, who had never seen the lady before in her life, advised
the woman not to sell because her husband would be home in
time to share a Christmas celebration. Well, Christmas came
and her husband was still in prison. But suddenly the case took
an unexpected turn, and the appellate court freed the man.
They celebrated the following Christmas together.

Over the years Rosanna has made some amazing predictions, some of which she made in my presence or to reputable witnesses who have testified accordingly. Here are several of the most outstanding.

On July 19, 1973, Rosanna predicted that "Nixon may get out of the Watergate affair elegantly by resigning." Nixon resigned August 7, 1973.

On January 10, 1990, Rosanna stated "I see a 707 airplane, approaching the Atlantic coast, crashing. I perceive digits...5?" On January 26, 1990, Aviancas Colombia's airline, flight 52, a Boeing 707, crashed trying to land at Kennedy airport.

Rosanna predicted on September 23, 1983 that "the United States and the Soviet Union will recognize the need to work together in unison as danger mounts from nations with nothing to lose, such as Iran, Iraq, and Libya." In the summer of 1990 the United States and the Soviet Union were "chummy" as never before, and worries concerning Iraq and Iran are greater than ever.

During the summer of 1989, Rosanna, whom I had been monitoring carefully as to her accuracy for thirteen years, insisted that all was not well with the president and his family. She insisted there were health problems and we would hear about them soon, as well as other problems which were even more worrisome concerning his immediate family. On January 10, 1990, she put her concerns in writing to me. How accurate was this? On February 15, 1990, Barbara Bush had surgery on her lip and also had a problem with her eyes. On January 29, 1990, Neil Bush, the president's son, began having business problems mounting to ominous proportions, and on April 12, 1990, the president discovered signs of glaucoma.

On January 10, 1990, Rosanna Rogers stated to me that "the Demjanjuk case will get a new twist, they've got the wrong man." For a European woman with horrible memories of the Hitler era, predicting the innocence of a man accused of being a concentration camp guard and war criminal placed her professional integrity above her personal feelings. While the world watched the trial in Israel of "Ivan the Terrible," as Demjanjuk was called, no one doubted the outcome for the accused man, who was known to be a particularly vicious and murderous villain. Demjanjuk and his lawyer insisted all along that he was the victim of mistaken identity and he was not "Ivan the Terrible," as accused.

Personally, I doubted Rosanna's prediction, but events proved my suspicions wrong and Rosanna's predictions to be right.

On February 26, 1990, Polish villagers who lived near the former Treblinka concentration camp told reporters from the news show *60 Minutes* that the name of the man who had been dubbed "Ivan the Terrible" was Marczenco, *not* Demjanjuk.

On February 28, 1990, Ohio congressman J. Trafficant, in whose district Demjanjuk had lived for many years, began to champion his cause. On May 14, 1990, the Israeli court heard an appeal on the man's death sentence, which had been imposed by the lower court. As a result, the Demjanjuk case was reopened, and a new investigation overturned the previous conviction and the man was set free. He quickly returned to the United States and currently lives a very quiet life.

Concerning less serious predictions, Rosanna stated to me during 1988 and 1989 that the millionaire real estate developer Donald Trump was heading for a "fall." On January 10, 1990, she said, "he will learn the raw fear of losses, both emotionally and in business, but he will bounce back." On the same day, Rosanna assured me that former president Reagan would be the first president in American history to testify in court. He did, in February and March of that year.

I have known and worked with Rosanna since the 1970s and consider her the most knowledgeable tarot reader in the world. She is, in addition, a gifted psychic, even without the use of her cards. The tarot deck Rosanna designed and uses is unlike any other ever created, and draws upon mythology as symbolism. Rosanna has also written a handbook with explanations concerning the use of this very special, very accurate card deck only available through her. Rosanna Rogers gives incredibly accurate readings by telephone as well as in person.

Schuler, Carol
70 East 10th Street
New York, NY 10003
Tel.: 212-473-2086

Carol Schuler is a fine reader, using both cards and her psychic abilities to give accurate predictions for her clients. Some of her most profound cases include the following:

During a reading with Ms. M., Carol told her client that she would marry a man from another country. A year later Ms. M. met and married a man from Ireland.

Carol told Ms. A. that she would be married and have a child within two years. Two years later the client returned with the news that the prediction had come true.

A very pregnant Ms. A. went to Carol for a reading. During the session she was told that her child would be a little girl, even though her doctor and all of her family and friends predicted a boy. Needless to say, Ms. A. had a girl.

Ms. D. asked Carol if she would get a raise that had been promised. Carol told her client that she would not get it because the man who had promised it to her would no longer be working there when the raise was due. Six months later there was a major reorganization of the company, and her boss, who had promised her the raise, was out.

Carol once told Ms. R. that she would be married in two years, but not to her current boyfriend. This prediction also came to pass.

During a reading, Ms. E. told Carol she had discovered

her husband in bed with their maid and wanted to know if she should divorce him. Carol told her no, stating that she would be able to speak with her husband and work things out. A few months later the client told Carol that she had followed her advice, that things were better between them, and that she was happy she had not done anything impulsive.

Carol Schuler sees private clients in addition to having regular sessions at a local cafe.

Sherman, Johanna
P.O. Box 240148
Brooklyn, NY 11224
Tel.: 718-373-9867

Johanna Sherman, the designer and creator of the Sacred Rose Tarot deck, has been one of the best known and busiest readers in the New York metropolitan area.

If one is able to obtain an appointment with Ms. Sherman, she will astound you with some very accurate and concrete information concerning yourself and the future. I met Johanna in 1978 through a friend and her readings have proven to be both accurate and specific, and many of her predictions have come true.

I consider Johanna to be a major psychic, and some examples of her powerful readings follow.

A client sought out Johanna for a reading during which the psychic included a warning where she "saw" something of "physical violence of a sexual nature" happening to the client's daughter on a family estate. Johanna couldn't speak of the horror of the situation; but the word "rape" stuck in her throat. The client's daughter, unaware of her mother's reading, was violated and raped on the way home from evening classes.

Once, while giving readings to a group of women, Johanna read a card spread for a woman in which she foretold dire circumstances. The cards suggested "female problems and health issues" and that the woman's health was not as it should be, so Johanna suggested the woman go to her gynecologist for an exam as soon as possible. The reading did not impress the woman and she dismissed the warning, telling Johanna that she had been to her doctor only one month ago and was pronounced in perfect health. A week or so went by before Johanna heard from one of the woman's friends that the lady had been taken away in an ambulance, hemorrhaging as a result of a fibroid tumor. It seems that her doctor had taken a "wait and see" attitude with her condition and did not realize the precarious condition his patient was in until she was taken to the hospital.

On another occasion, Johanna predicted a woman would meet a tall, light-haired man with the initial D in his name, who would be close to her age and would be involved in a different type of occupation as an authority; he would possess a very expensive leather attaché case with rounded edges. The psychic also said that the actor David Soul kept coming up and that the woman would be involved in business with this person. The woman called later to say that she indeed met a tall, light-haired man with a resemblance to the actor David Soul. His last name began with the letter D, and he owned a gem business dealing with expensive diamonds and other stones. When the man traveled, he carried his stones in his leather attaché with soft edges. During the reading Johanna had also mentioned the possibility that her client might travel to Egypt or somewhere in the Middle East. It turned out that the man did travel to the Middle East for business and she might have the occasion to travel with him. Johanna has also made previous predictions for this client which materialized.

Johanna Sherman gives readings by mail and by telephone (arrangements for telephone readings must be made in advance). Johanna believes that a tarot reading should initiate change for the better. Many times her readings are eye-opening but do not always give the information the client had hoped for; nevertheless Johanna gives the information as she perceives it, and usually it is extraordinarily accurate.

Sisson, Pat
6828 Reddeye Road
Knoxville, TN 37918
Tel.: 423-689-4469

I have known Pat since 1985, when she was already well-known in Tennessee as a reliable psychic reader and counselor. Pat is a true medium, has been involved in ghost-hunting activities, and also conducts seminars and lectures—often for business organizations, various civic groups, and clubs.

While doing a reading for Art, an investigator and inventor, Pat predicted he would be suddenly contacted and added to an organization and, as a result, would travel overseas and meet several foreign professionals, two of whom would become friends; one would be from Canada and the other from England. Two months later the client reported that he was appointed to an international team and had consequently traveled and worked overseas for several months.

During another session, Pat predicted Jeanie, whose husband managed a resort, would win a large amount of money, more than Jeanie had ever seen at once. Several months later the couple won $4 million at a casino in Tennessee.

While reading for Nancy, a cosmetic representative, Pat predicted that Nancy would not marry the man she was currently dating but would accidentally run into the sister of an old classmate from high school and rekindle their friendship, and would then marry the classmate's brother within three months. The client was somewhat upset by this news. However, two months later she telephoned Pat to invite her to her wedding to the classmate's brother. She and the classmate had not seen each other for over twenty years.

In another instance Pat predicted a client would sell her

house three weeks before she even had listed the house for sale. The house sold the very day it was listed.

Taylor, Valerie Svolos
951 Ontario
Shreveport, LA 71106

Tel.: 318-861-0930
Valerie Svolos Taylor has a devoted following of clients from all over the world. Some of her more accurate predictions are as follows.

Gillian M. met Valerie in the fall of 1992. During the reading Valerie was able to pinpoint the client's stomach problem and identify the husband's profession. She also predicted a career in media for the woman, who now works in radio.

During another session Valerie was able to accurately predict that the United States would bomb Iraq several years before the actual event.

During one reading Valerie kept insisting that her client would receive between $1,500 to $2,000 in the mail. The client adamantly declared it impossible. Several weeks passed before the client telephoned to report that she had received $1,800 in the mail for an oil lease.

Three years ago a young woman went to see Valerie about her two sons. The psychic reported that she "saw" three children around the woman, two boys and a girl. The woman stated that she had no intention of having other children. Sometime later the client gave birth to a baby girl.

An insurance executive, who was Valerie's client for over five years, had been told for several weeks that there were problems in the accounting area of the business. The man checked but didn't find anything wrong. Then the CEO of the company resigned and the other executives found evidence of his embezzlement of money from the firm.

During a visit with a friend in Tampa last summer, Valerie

advised a coworker of her friend not to buy a new house, as she was thinking of doing, but to wait because she would meet someone new and would be moving to South Carolina. Both women laughed in disbelief. Later that year during a visit at Christmas, Valerie's friend told her that the woman had, as predicted, met a man and moved to South Carolina.

A businessman from New Orleans telephoned Valerie to inquire about two men with whom he was thinking of going into business. She advised the man against it, saying that she had bad feelings about the two men and that there was criminal activity involved. The man ignored the psychic's advice and invested anyway. The two partners subsequently went to prison and the businessman lost his investment.

Several years ago Valerie gave a woman a reading who was very involved with a married man. Valerie advised the woman to drop him, as she saw many wives and entanglements around him. In the months following the reading, the woman reported that she had heard from three different women involved with the man, all claiming to be his wife!

In another instance during a session, Valerie told a client, who was leaving for New York City the following day, that she would purchase a yellow blazer during her trip. The woman called Valerie on the second day to say that she had bought a blazer, but a red one, teasing Valerie. However, the following day, the woman had to recant because she discovered a flaw in the first jacket, returned it to the store to find that the only color left was yellow, and so ended up with the yellow blazer Valerie originally predicted.

A mother went to Valerie worried because she had been unable to contact her son. During the reading Valerie kept sensing blood and death around the woman's son. Sadly the following day the police had to enter the son's house by breaking down the door and found that he had committed suicide.

Valerie gave a reading to a young woman who was completely devastated by the death of her husband from a car accident. During the reading Valerie "heard" the woman's husband say that the accident did not happen as the police believed and that there was another car involved that had fled the scene. Valerie urged the woman to find an attorney and to hire a private detective. As a result, the full truth of the events that caused the accident were discovered and the woman received a settlement large enough to provide for her and her children for life.

Once during a visit of Valerie's sister and her kids, the children asked to have Greek coffee and to have their coffee grounds (left over in the cup) read. Her sister picked up her cup and said, "Read this cup first." The first thing Valerie "saw" was water rising. The sister thought she was teasing because of her insistence to be read first. Valerie stated, "No, I insist your house is flooded." The sister then telephoned a neighbor who was house sitting, and the woman declared that she had been trying to locate her all day to tell her that her house was flooded!

Wagner, Chuck
4 Park Avenue
New York, NY 10016
Tel.: 212-725-8849

A very good tarot reader and nice man, Chuck is often very accurate and specific, obviously possessing considerable psychic ability. Chuck has a large entertainment business clientele, but also works for corporations and gives private readings, as well as teaching tarot interpretation.

Some of Mr. Wagner's more specific predictions related to me follow.

Once Mr. Wagner predicted that a client would go into a business venture with a friend and lose both her investment and the friendship. The client returned the following year, saying that she felt her reading had been a wasted investment since what had been predicted was so far-fetched; she had a good job and had no intention of going into business with anyone. However, later a friend did convince her to open a retail clothing business, and she lost her investment and the friendship exactly as predicted several years earlier.

"One of my clients (M.B.) came to find out how her anticipated divorce from a man she described as verbally and sometimes physically abusive, bitter, cruel, insensitive, resentful, and disdainful, would turn out.... Her husband threatened to fight her in court. Her two children from this thirty-year marriage were both adults. The reading indicated that she should be patient, prayerful, and practical. I told her that the tarot reading indicated she stay put and redirect her thinking away from her pain to whatever projects she could find to keep busy, and then she would emerge victorious. But if she tried to divorce him, it would be costly and she would endure much pain and hardship and have to struggle to make ends meet. She followed the suggestions. Eighteen months later her husband passed away. She prospered and went on to build a happy life."

In another instance, "R.S.M., a female client, had been indicted by a grand jury for masterminding the theft of a half million dollars worth of blank money orders from a major bank. Two men, who had been arrested trying to sell the money orders to an undercover agent, were given total immunity and testified that R.S.M. had stolen the documents. This woman came for a reading to discover the best way to handle herself and to find out what the outcome of the trial would be. The reading disclosed that she should plead "not guilty" and refuse to take the stand, which she did against her lawyer's recommendation to plead guilty in exchange for a guaranteed period of probation. There was a claim that her thumbprint was found on one of the documents and she would definitely be convicted. She trusted the reading and was found not guilty by the jury."

During a reading, Chuck advised a certain female to go out with her friend because she would meet her future husband. She did, but met someone she found to be totally unacceptable. However, over time she grew to like and then love the man and eventually the two moved in together and got married.

J.M. went to Chuck anxious about getting pregnant and successfully delivering a baby. Chuck told her not to worry and that she would have twins. When the woman became pregnant, her doctor told her she definitely wasn't having twins, but when she delivered, much to her doctor's surprise, there were two babies instead of one.

Winner, Joyce
4173 S. Binshal Place
Tulsa, OK 74105
Tel.: 918-744-9411

Joyce Winner has a good reputation both as a psychic and healer. Presently residing in Tulsa, Oklahoma, Joyce also occasionally works at a local Spiritualist Church.

I first met Joyce in 1976, and in October 1977 she had the courage to predict my marriage ending, along with the reasons why. She was right.

During another meeting in January 1979, she spoke of my writing something "about a Loch Ness monster." I did, years later. Also during the same reading she told me that I would travel to California where I would meet a woman I would become close to, even giving the woman's unusual family name, which also proved accurate.

On May 22, 1980, she described a scene where she "saw" me with a woman named Elaine, in California, at the ocean, with other people. A few years later, in 1984, I did spend an evening at a well-known actress's house on the Pacific, and my date was named Elaine.

Joyce also accurately forecast in June 1982 that some of my books would be reprinted. This also came about in 1986, four years later.

Joyce currently lives with her husband in Tulsa and gives personal readings.

Yolana
245 East 58th Street
New York, NY 10022
Tel.: 212-308-0836

Truly the queen of psychics, Yolana can be so accurate and detailed that one wonders how it is possible. Living in a building named Le Triomphe, she triumphs in her readings with a detail that only the most gifted of psychics would be able to do. With a long list of would-be clients, she is able to eventually see all of them.

Yolana had amazing powers even as a small child; when she was ten she would mentally make the doorbell ring when she wanted to go outside. Her mother was a Hungarian gypsy who read cards for friends, so it is possible she inherited some of her mother's abilities.

When I first worked with Yolana, the psychic world was new and mysterious to her. Now almost twenty years later, she is usually right on target with her predictions. In 1971 Yolana told a neighbor in Eastchester, New York, not to date a certain man because he would die of a heart attack while driving; he did, and the neighbor never doubted Yolana since. Some of her other amazing predictions follow.

On November 12, 1978, Yolana "saw" a silver and blue railroad train derail, with a lot of injuries as a result; something would go wrong with the tracks at the end of November or in early December. On December 3, the Southern Railway Express derailed near Charlottesville, Virginia, killing six and injuring more than forty, just as she had described.

On December 2, 1978, Yolana predicted the "collapse of a building in a busy part of New York City within two weeks." On December 17, a scaffolding on a Fifth Avenue apartment building collapsed, narrowly missing crowds.

On December 19, 1978, Yolana told me of an airplane crash "over hills in the suburban United States." She told me that there would be trouble with the left wing and that there would be casualties and the figure 7 was somehow connected. The following day a small plane crashed in a suburban area on the West Coast, the left wing hitting a tree while crashing. Of the six people on the plane and one on the ground involved, there was only one survivor.

On January 11, 1979, Yolana stated that "one Oriental country would invade another very shortly." China surprised the world by invading Vietnam on February 17, 1979.

In January 1979 she predicted that a disco in New York City would be engulfed in flames due to candles. The fire occurred in mid-February.

On January 16, 1979, Yolana spoke of a "terror ride" on a train going to Coney Island. On February 26, a man terrorized and victimized passengers on just such a train.

On December 17, 1978, Yolana told me she foresaw a bombing at a busy New York terminal shortly after New Year's Day, with many hurt, the work of a crazy person and not politically motivated. On February 19, 1979, three teenagers set fire to a subway token booth, and as a result three people died. The motive was personal revenge.

On November 15, 1980, Yolana confided in her secretary, Rose, the gist of a vision in which she saw someone in terrible danger near black gates; a man getting out of a car, someone will be killed, it is very big—"I hear many shots."

She thought someone named David was involved, and also said that a name like "Lemon" kept running through her mind. Three days later, John Lennon was shot by a man named Mark David Chapman in front of the black gates of the Dakota Building in New York City where he lived.

When psychics give predictions, the timing predicted is not always accurate. On May 9, 1980, Yolana spoke to me of Waldenbooks in respect to my writing. That company became my publisher twelve years later.

On October 15, 1985, Yolana predicted an earthquake near San Bernardino, California, that would also be felt in New York. The event took place exactly as predicted February 18, 1986.

During the same time, Yolana also spoke of a bombing by the PLO at a military base in Germany, but was not sure of the place name, which she thought sounded like "Bogen." A nightclub in Berlin frequented by U.S. military personnel was bombed by Arab terrorists on October 24.

Yolana makes her living by giving personal readings to individuals, not by making world predictions. During sessions she is given to rattling off names connected with a client, many of whom the client only learns of or meets later.

On March 14, 1989, during a reading I had with her, Yolana named David, Stephanie, Susan; people whom I later met. In addition she also remarkably named Newhouse, whom I met in 1993—four years later. Readings often contain names and situations that do not make any sense at the time; she named twelve names I could not identify on October 25, 1990, eight of whom I subsequently met, some of which became important connections.

After recovering from a bout of illness that forced Yolana to work less, she is now back at full speed. During our first meeting after more than a year's separation, she overwhelmed me with names she could not have known and predicted that there might be major changes in my career and life.

This brings up a question often asked of me: Does a psychic "read" a client's mind and thereby name people and situations known to the client; in other words, giving not a prediction but merely a mind-reading? Not so. I contend that physics "read" the person's destiny field or whatever term one wishes to give to the aura containing information about that person's future, often referred to as the akashic records, the world mind, or what I sometimes call "the personal floppy disk."

On January 20, 1994, Yolana quite spontaneously confronted me with a statement just as I entered her apartment about Canada and a television project involving me and Canada, the names David and Ben, and a book of mine which she identified as "Amityville"! As a matter of fact, I had just signed an agreement, through my agent Ben, with a producer named David, about a series of films based on my Amityville books. Consequently I confirmed this information with Yolana, telling her that a French company was going to produce these films. She immediately replied, "Oh no, not just a French company, several other countries are also involved." Since this was not what I had been told, I checked with the producer, who confirmed that indeed several other countries were involved. Yolana had not read my mind because this was information I did not even know.

In addition to private readings, Yolana helps police solve crimes free of charge. According to Lieutenant Riguzzi of the Harrison, New York, homicide squad, Yolana's abilities are amazing, and he offers her the highest praise. A double murder of two young girls in 1984 was solved largely due to Yolana's insights. When impressed with information concerning a murder, for instance, she submerges into a trancelike state, which she is unable to recall later. It appears that in some cases, the deceased supply her with information. In one case she stated during a trance, "I lost one of my cufflinks." This turned out to be the case: the body was found with a cufflink missing.

In another police case, Yolana stated that the victim "had something wrong with his ring finger." When the body was found, it appeared the murderer could not remove a valuable ring, so he cut off the finger!

In her private readings, Yolana deals with far gruesome matters. Still, she says what she "sees" and does not edit the information to "soften the blow" for the client. Det. Thomas McCue, of Greenwich, Connecticut, confirms that Yolana, upon meeting a colleague with the first name Bill and just married, stated that the marriage would last two years and then break up. The marriage lasted two years and three days.

Yolana has read for celebrities, statesmen, and the like. Even though there may be a wait for her services because of the demand, it is well worth the experience.

Outside of the U.S.

Al Huneidi, Sahar H.
23 Chesterfield House
South Audley, London
W14 57B England
Tel.: 44-171-493-8364
Fax: 44-171-495-1476

Sahar has, over a period of two years, accurately predicted matters pertaining to my career that were of immense value, and without ever meeting me. She has also given many accurate predictions for a friend of mine, Paula R., who takes them very seriously.

Sahar was originally trained by the psychic Merryn Jose, the daughter of famed psychic Maureen Traynor, also from London. Sahar has never shied away from giving accurate predictions, even if they turn out to be negative, such as in delicate matters of the heart. Her predictions have proven to be very beneficial in the long run for most of her clients.

Gardner, Richard
10 Sudeley Street
Brighton BN2 1HE, England
Tel.: 44-273-683-211

Richard Gardner, living in the wonderful town of Brighton, is one of England's best psychics.

I have known Mr. Gardner nearly twenty years, and my sessions with him have always proven to be revealing, accurate, and very personal. He has written several very good books on paranormal subjects and uses a deck of cards for reading designed by an English artist; cards which in no way resemble any of the current tarot decks.

Gaudy, John
1212 Forsyth Street
Glebe 2037
New South Wales, Australia
Tel.: 61-2037-660-5647

John Gaudy was formerly a successful actor, though he always knew that he had considerable psychic ability. He eventually became a professional reader, both in New York City and his native Australia, where he now resides. Mr. Gaudy has acquired a large following and become something of a media personality as well as a medium.

An honest, pleasant person, Mr. Gaudy yielded high results of accuracy when tested, and he has a devoted clientele who swear by him.

Hearne, Ronald
Tel.: 44-171-622-6857

Ronald Hearne, who is one of the best psychics now active in England, and whom I have known for years, is both a reader and a deep-trance medium. In the latter capacity, he worked with me on the case of the Nell Gwynn house in Soho, citing evidence that could only have come from the late lady of Charles II.

Montgomery, Pauline (Maddock)
529 Shan Road
Royton, Oldham
Lancashire, England
Tel.: 44-706-849-411

For many years Pauline has been active as a spiritualist and psychic reader, having a considerable psychic gift and following. Among the many roles she plays are counselor, lecturer, and psychic artist (she receives impressions from communicating entities and interprets them on paper).

Solomon, Philip
8 Marshall Road
Willenhall, West Midlands
WV13 32QD England
Tel.: 44-1902-830-200
Cel.: 44-0585-130281

One of the handful of truly great mediums of this century, Philip Solomon belongs among the ranks of Yolana and the late Eileen Garrett and Ethel Johnson Meyers.

Since my first contact with him several years ago, he has been so incredibly evidential with names, connections, and situations concerning information that he would in no way have access to, that I can only marvel at his gift.

In addition, Mr. Solomon is a good writer, with several

books published in the U.K. He is also a popular radio personality and lecturer.

Without knowing anything about me or the books I have published, Mr. Solomon sent me a fax in which he was able to name my late mother and even the unusual spelling of her name; he also asked if I knew of a priest named Father Leo— my *father* was named Leo!

Philip recently sent me another fax in which he stated that a Christina along with a Peter M. were important for me. He had no knowledge that my agent was named Christina and that we were negotiating with a Peter Mayer about a new book!

Mr. Solomon has also given a reading for a friend of mine, listing personal information, intimate family details, and named late family members and their manners of death, without ever having met my friend.

Truly, Philip Solomon is the greatest trance medium I have ever known and an incredible psychic as well.

**Van Der Heide,
Jan Cornelius**
Rhi jngeesterstraatweg
12 2343 XC
Oegstgeest, The Netherlands
Tel.: 31-71-172-870

Highly literate and knowledgeable, Jan is both a psychic and a healer, and has been involved in the publication of magazines dealing with psychic phenomena in his native Holland. Mr. Van Der Heide also works as a hypnotherapist and is very well respected in Europe. In addition, while in trance, he paints portraits of spirits he senses, those who have passed on.

I visited with Mr. Van Der Heide in 1979, after hearing

of him the previous year. One of the best known of his written predictions occurred on September 13, 1978, when he stated that Pope John Paul I would not live long; he would be dead within four months. At that time the newly crowned Pope seemed in perfect health. Of course, events proved to be different and rumors of foul play have always been associated with his death.

On December 29, 1990, Mr. Van Der Heide stated on radio and in writing that "there will be a short and heavy war in the Middle East. I see American bombers fly to and above Baghdad." Further, he predicted that there would be a military coup in Russia, and that "Gorbatsjow will disappear from the scene in 1991." By Gorbatsjow he must have meant Gorbachev. He also predicted in great detail, including maps, an invasion by the Soviet Union of Germany, which never occurred. But who knows if it was planned but never executed and he may have picked up those thoughts?

In the Netherlands, Mr. Van Der Heide is widely respected and highly regarded. He is taken very seriously both as a "paragnost," or clairvoyant, and as an unusual painter.

5

HEALERS

Sometimes the gift of the psychic, of mediumship of one kind or another, comes hand in hand with the gift of healing. While resistance by the conservative establishment toward any kind of psychic practitioners has often been unyielding (and mainly due to lack of actual knowledge of the evidence), when it comes to healing, the resistance in some quarters becomes fierce and blindly intolerant. Fortunately, the attitude of the medical establishment is softening, and the United States government has recently established an office for the investigation of alternative medicine.

In view of so many incurable diseases haunting mankind these days, from herpes to AIDS to cancer and many more, anything that *works* ought to be welcome. Wisely, the best course is to combine the best of both worlds, traditional medicine with alternative ways for the benefit of the patient. Sometimes this will not work, because the approaches and philosophies behind each doctrine are at odds with one another.

Unorthodox treatment should never replace ordinary medical methods, except where a patient clearly prefers them—such as with some surgery, chemical treatments, antiobiotics—because the patient believes in "natural" ways of dealing with disease.

The basic difference between conventional medicine and the various forms of psychic healing has been summed up by

Dr. William McGarey, a medical doctor who heads the Edgar Cayce clinic in Phoenix, Arizona, where treatments according to Cayce's teachings and beliefs are available. "The way Cayce looked at it," Dr. McGarey explained to me, "an individual is first of all a *spiritual being,* and manifests, through mind, as a material being. The spirit creates and the physical body is the result. But in medicine we think of structure: a man has liver disease, or lung disease. The way Cayce saw it is that one of the forces within the body has become unbalanced with the other forces."

The Cayce approach to healing is based on the revelations by this amazing man, who was a simple photographer in life, but when in deep trance was able to diagnose at a distance and prescribe sometimes extremely intricate cures—knowledge he could not possibly possess in a waking condition. The Cayce readings have long become the basis of the Association for Research and Enlightenment in Virginia Beach, Va., a foundation where people can get information on a large number of ailments.

What exactly *is* psychic healing? If one is to grasp the significance of these seemingly impossible cures, one has to accept the duality of man as its rational basis: a physical body on the outside, but a finer, inner, or etheric body underneath, the real *persona,* the soul, if you wish. Psychic healing is always holistic: the entire person is healed, body and etheric body; one without the other cannot be treated.

A lot of confusion exists in the mind of the average person as to what psychic healing is and how it comes about—if it comes about.

There are a number of healing processes that differ from *currently* accepted medical practice. They are as old as mankind, and have existed in various forms and under various names since time immemorial. In ancient times, such healings were considered miraculous (or sometimes diabolic) and only in recent years has an orderly, reasonable, scientific approach become possible. Today, more and more members of the medical community are taking another look at these seemingly "impossible" cures, whereas a scant five or ten years ago the subject of alternative healing could not even be discussed or taken seriously.

First, there is *psychic healing* proper. Here the healer draws energy from his physical body, mainly from the two solar plexuses in back of the stomach and at the top of the head, where ganglia of nerves come together. This energy is then channeled through his hands and applied to the *aura* of the patient. A good healer notices a *discolored* aura (the magnetic field extending somewhat beyond the physical body). Discoloration indicates illness. By placing his energy into the troubled areas of the aura, the healer displaces the diseased particles and momentarily creates a vacuum. Into this vacuum rush healthy, electrically charged particles to fill the gap in the aura, and instant healing is the result, since the physical body must fall in line with its inner etheric counterpart.

This type of psychic healer—either a man or a woman, sometimes even a youngster, for the gift plays no favorites—rarely touches the patient's skin. The healing takes place at the periphery of the aura, where it is most sensitive. Healing may take place whether the patient believes in it or not. It is a purely mechanical process, and its success depends on the healer's ability to draw enough of his life force into his hands to affect the healing.

Psychic healers who are Spiritualists prefer to attribute their successes to the intervention of spirit controls, but I find that some non-Spiritualists and even some atheists have remarkable results.

Physical healing, the second kind of unorthodox treatment, consists of touching the body in the afflicted areas. This laying on of hands has been practiced by many religions, and even today it is at least symbolically part of church ritual. Although the prime force in this kind of treatment is still the psychic energy of the healer, a positive attitude toward it on the part of the patient is helpful, and when the healer is also a priest or minister, religious faith enters the process to some extent.

Hypnotherapy as a form of psychic healing is a method in which the patient undergoes deep hypnosis so that he or she may effect self-healing. The healer first explores emotional conflicts within the patient, removes them, and replaces them with positive, helpful *suggestions*. By placing such low-key commands into the unconscious mind of the patient, the hypnotic suggestions help the patient overcome his ailments using his own psychic energies in the process.

Faith healing is often confused in the public's mind with psychic healing, but it has little in common with it. In faith healing everything depends on three elements. First, the afflicted person must have a religious belief in the power of healing (and in the intercession of divine forces), the more fanatical, the better. Second, the patient must have unlimited confidence in the healer from whom he expects "the miracle." Third, a large audience, the larger the better, is a must for the faith healing to succeed. The late Katherine Kuhlman is a prime example of an acclaimed faith healer. She never took credit for the considerable number of cures taking place right in front of the crowd, but hinted at divine will working through her as the originator of the seeming miracle.

But successful faith healings are not necessarily the results of religious belief alone. In invoking spiritual guidance, the faith healer unleashes within himself psychic forces that are utilized to heal the sick; the hopeful state in which the usually desperate patient finds himself often pitched at the point of hysteria, in turn spurs his *own* healing powers to higher performance, and so the result may be spontaneous cure. The reservoir of human psychic energy represented by the large audience is also drawn upon to supply additional power for the process.

Bernardo, Cesar
Tel.: 212-567-8811

Mr. Bernardo is a Philippine psychic now residing in New York City. Mr. Bernardo has gained a good reputation, having made accurate predictions in his native country for years.

Mr. Bernardo has the ability to identify areas of illness in people, but he is not a healer, in that he leaves treating the condition to medical doctors. I met Mr. Bernardo in 1994 through a mutual friend, Alfred, who had been impressed with Bernardo's abilities.

One of his amazing abilities includes "reading" cases from the past. Situations are suggested to him, and he provides additional details with which he could not be familiar.

Blake, Mary
166 West 72nd Street
New York, NY 10023
Tel.: 212-724-4081

Mary Blake is a gifted healer with a long track record of helping people to her credit. In addition to her healing ability, she is also a gifted psychic and has developed a remarkable gift that allows her to make people regress into their past lives. Trained by reputable organizations in the skills of hypnosis and healing, she has authored numerous articles on the subject. Mary also teaches spiritual and healing development.

Collins, Doris
Tel.: 44-171-948-3316

Doris Collins is known as an active healer and organizer of seminars on healing in her native England. Ms. Collins is also a fine psychic and her life story was recently published as a successful book titled *A Woman of Spirit: The Autobiography of a Psychic*.

Cooper, Maria
521 Park Avenue
New York, NY 10021

Maria Cooper, the daughter of the late actor Gary Cooper, is a well-established healer, though her activities are better known as a dedicated proponent of psychic healing and alternative medicine.

Dye, Betty
P.O. Box 69
Union, GA 30291
Tel.: 770-969-9431

Betty Dye, a homemaker, has an innate gift of healing that appeared spontaneously. She is one of perhaps a dozen reputable psychic healers in the country who have been gaining a reputation for helping people in situations where traditional medical care has failed.

James, an author and officer of the local chapter of the Theosophical Society, consulted Betty about a stomach ailment; however Betty had no knowledge of the condition. Immediately Betty went into a trance, during which one of her "controls," who had been a medical doctor while alive, diagnosed James's ailment as stomach trouble, speaking through Betty, and instructed the medium telepathically to place her hands upon the client's stomach. The client had been in continual pain up to that moment; however, it subsided immediately. He left the session pain-free, and the pain did not recur.

In another instance Mrs. C. went to Betty in a state of fear because her doctor had diagnosed a growth in her throat, and surgery was necessary to remove it. The client related the following: "The day before surgery I went to see Betty Dye, who gave me psychic healing. During the treatment I experienced a wonderful feeling of cleansing and extreme heat coming from the hands of the medium while she was in a trance. When I went to the doctor afterward, the growth had completely disappeared and it has not come back since."

Guidice, Lena
Tel.: 718-648-8891

Lena Guidice is a Brooklyn-based Italian healer who has a very good reputation among the Italian community.

Healing Light Center
261 East Allegro Avenue, Suite 12
Sierra Madre, CA 91204
Tel.: 818-306-2710
Fax: 818-355-0966

The Healing Light Center, founded by Rosalyn Bruyere, is an organization of healers who specialize in certain ailments or parts of the body. The group is compartmentalized in that once a condition is identified, the client is referred to the best practitioner for that specific ailment.

Kolman, Ze'ev
250 West 57th Street, Suite 630
New York, NY 10017
Tel.: 212-245-1715

In 1960, Ze'ev Kolman was stationed at a base called Uhom Hasiba in the Sinai desert as part of his military service. At 4 A.M., restless, he decided to take a walk up a mountain near the base. There he had a close encounter with a UFO, and *unaccountably* lost a great deal of time during which he must have been on that mountain. When he returned to the base, he was a different man. He discovered that the touch of his hand caused electrical discharges to the extent that people he touched experienced the equivalent of an electric shock. Soon Kolman discovered he could heal the sick, and gradually this quiet, ordinary businessman—his family owned a dry goods store—became Israel's most famous psychic healer. People from all walks of life have consulted him, and many were cured of illnesses that ordinary medical treatment had failed to cure. Hollywood celebrities, major politicians in Washington and elsewhere, and a vast and increasing number of ordinary people have flocked to this man because he has indeed healed the sick in so many cases, sometimes with a single treatment.

I have told this man's full story, with all the evidence of his healing work, in my book *The Secret of Healing* (Beyond Words Publisher, 1996).

Kolman himself is not a cultist or religious fanatic. He is a man dedicated to scientific exploration of the gift he refers to as *bioenergy,* or life force, since the power is derived not from some extraterrestrial force (though that may have unleashed it originally) or from spirit intervention, but from his own, somehow "activated," physical body.

"I personally experienced his therapy and was truly impressed," stated Barry D. Mink, an internist practicing in Aspen, Colorado. The late singer John Denver wrote to

Kolman after a session: "I experienced a great increase in physical energy, mental clarity...."

Prince Alfred von Liechtenstein, president of the Vienna International Academy for the Study of the Future, asked Kolman to treat a close friend, a lady who had suffered serious eye damage from experimental extended-wear gas-permeable contact lenses and was in great pain. The lady received three treatments from Ze'ev Kolman within a span of two weeks, at the end of which she was completely cured.

"I am personally familiar with Mr. Kolman's ability as a healer," stated Senator Claiborne Pell. Dr. Enrique J. Teuscher, diplomate in psychiatry and a practicing neurologist, wrote that Ze'ev Kolman "is a bioenergist of extraordinary ability."

Among the many cases Kolman has successfully treated were cancerous tumors, a punctured lung, broken bones, and lost hearing, and nearly all types of illnesses and medical problems for which conventional medicine could provide no relief.

Kraft, Dean
Tel.: 212-358-3677

Formerly a musician, Mr. Kraft discovered his supernormal abilities by accident in November 1972. While driving home from work he heard a strange clicking sound and discovered the car doors had locked, even though he had not touched any of the appropriate buttons. As a joke, he asked out loud if there were any spirits present, and to his amazement, his answer was a series of clicks in some type of code. At the time he was working in a music shop, and together with his boss, they worked on understanding this code until he could actually communicate with "them."

One day he heard the horrible sounds of an automobile crash outside of the shop, so he rushed out to find a woman lying on the pavement who was obviously very hurt. Something told him to hold her in his hands until an ambulance arrived to take her to the hospital. Later that evening while driving home, the unseen communicators, via the code of clicks, communicated that "tonight your hands were used for healing." He did not understand the message, but when he checked on the woman's condition, the hospital told him that she was in critical condition and was scheduled for surgery the following morning. Upon telephoning the hospital the following morning, he was shocked to find that she had been released. He was told that somehow her injuries had "healed themselves during the early hours of the morning."

Today, and many years later, Kraft is extremely busy. He does not advertise his services, and his clients find him by word of mouth. Many of his clients are referred by doctors, whom he frequently works with. He often visits clients in the hospital with their doctors' approval. One doctor whom he helped (and who later says he was cured) was so impressed with his ability that he helped Kraft to organize a not-for-profit organization called the Foundation for Psycho-energetic Research. Frequently a doctor is present when he administers treatments, which he begins by slightly darkening the room, then proceeding to touch the patient's head and neck gently; during this stage of the treatment, Kraft feels he is "charging up his batteries." The healing lasts approximately five minutes, but afterwards Kraft needs to rest awhile, claiming that the sessions take a lot of energy.

Kraft has had particularly good success with psoriasis, tumors, and some forms of cancer. He enjoys doing laboratory research to discover more about his amazing powers.

His powers have sometimes worked miracles. One time he was called to North Shore Community Hospital to visit a patient who was dying of colon cancer. Kraft saw the man a couple of times, and today that man is still alive. A judge visited Kraft complaining of an incurable arthritic condition of his knees and back; after several treatments the man has remained pain-free to this day.

Kraft insists on checking up on his clients after seeing them in order to monitor their progress. He also teaches his methods, claiming that others can acquire his ability. Dr. Michael Smith of Lincoln Hospital in the Bronx, New York, has been using Kraft's method successfully; so has neurologist Dr. Gabriel Rubin. Psychiatrist Dr. Abraham Weinberg of New York considers the psychic healing demonstrated by Dean Kraft a "valuable adjunct" to conventional medical treatment.

Kraft administers his healing by a "laying on of hands" method with overwhelming and lasting results. Representatives Julia Howard of the North Carolina State Legislature, witnessed her husband, who was suffering from a medically incurable sclerosis, become symptom-free after receiving Kraft's treatments. Dr. Dorothea B. Chapman's cancer was arrested after Kraft's touch therapy. Clearly, something physical happens to the client after being touched by Kraft. According to Brian G.M. Durie, M.D., who is a professor of medicine at UCLA and Cedars-Sinai Medical Center and a cancer specialist, what Kraft does is an energy transfer, and worthy of further studies.

Kraft and his wife and partner, Rochelle, wrote a book, *A Touch of Hope* (Putnam, 1998), that tells Kraft's story. Dean Kraft is well on his way to following in the footsteps of the late famed healer John Myers.

Krystal, Phyllis
The Aura Bookshop
Los Angeles, CA
Tel.: 213-656-9373

Phyllis Krystal is a fine healer whom I wrote about in my book *Healing Beyond Medicine*. She is a very private person, but she and her husband have healed cancer patients, one of whom I know personally.

Lucas, Heidi
Pfluegerstrasse 86
4 Dusseldorf 33 Germany
Tel.: 49-211-612-623

Heidi Lucas, a good German healer, spent many years in Indonesia, where she studied her craft with the best Indonesian healers and teachers.

Poyel, Eliane
Tel.: 212-683-5075

Eliane Poyel, originally from France, is a healer who specializes in Reiki and the "laying on of hands." She has studied with Canadian masters and has practiced her art both in France and in the United States.

Purpora, Maureen
Tel.: 212-288-3028

Maureen Purpora has been a psychic reader for over twenty years both in the United States and in Europe, for which she uses normal playing cards. In addition, Ms. Purpora is a professional Shiatsu massage therapist. She has combined her psychic work with her physical therapy work for the past ten years and has become adept at recognizing physical imbalances in the body as well as becoming a good healer. On our first meeting she was able to correctly describe the symptoms of a medical condition of mine—without previous knowledge. She can also give readings by telephone and she is bilingual (French and English).

6

PAGANS AND WITCHES

An integral part of practicing the ancient craft of Wicca is the study of astrology and divination. Many witches' covens have a resident psychic, many priests and priestesses of Wicca and members of other pagan groups work to develop psychic abilities.

Witches do not perform miracles or sacrifice anything except maybe their time on a grueling day at the job. They do practice a very ancient religion based upon naturalism, which has helped many to lead happier and more meaningful lives.

Adams, Frederick McLauren
12318 Shady Lane
Nevada City, CA 95959
Tel.: 530-265-2637

Frederick Adams is the creator and leader of Feraferia, one of the least known but most meaningful polytheistic movements. This movement is a blend of the ancient Minoan cults of Crete and Celtic beliefs and practices. I wrote about his work and organization extensively in *The New Pagans*. Those seeking an understanding of the deeper meanings and connections between man and the universe will find this man and his teachings to be enlightening and of great impact.

de Arechaga, Frederick (Ordun)
The Sabaean Religious Order
1420 Polyhynna St.
New Orleans, LA 70130
Tel.: 504-523-9514

Frederick de Arechaga, a very knowledgeable, cultured gentleman and Basque nobleman, came to the United States years ago via Cuba, settling in Chicago with his mother. By profession Mr. de Arechaga is an artist, but by avocation a researcher in the field of pagan religions and history. Eventually Mr. de Arechaga became the high priest of a very colorful temple devoted to the ancient Babylonian religion known as Sabaean. In addition, he owns an occult shop called El Saba and is probably one of the most erudite scholars in the field of ancient pre-Christian cults and religions. He refers to his own psychic work as the "opening of the oracle of Om."

People who have had sessions with him have reported him to be very accurate. At one time Frederic was also inducted into the sacred rituals of the Yoruba people of West Africa and thus received the name of Ordun.

Curott, Phyllis
Tel.: 212-663-5642

A successful attorney by profession, Ms. Curott is also the head of a highly esoteric group of Wiccans. Phyllis does not seek publicity, but practices her craft with a small group of dedicated devotees. Those who are interested in Wicca will find her very helpful.

Enchantments
341 East 9th Street
New York, NY 10003
Tel.: 212-228-4394

Enchantments is not a person, but a very interesting shop in Manhattan's East Village selling occult supplies ranging from books, candles, and jewelry, to incense and witchcraft paraphernalia of all kinds.

Among the staff, who are followers of the Wiccan religion, are always one or two professional psychics who give readings and are very knowledgeable concerning the paranormal. The manager of Enchantments is Carol, who is adept in the art and religion of Wicca.

Morgana
311 Hardis Road
Warwick, RI 02880

Morgana is the head of a highly regarded coven in Rhode Island.

Runyon, Carroll
P.O. Box 403
Silverado, CA 92676
Fax.: 714-649-4456

Carroll Runyon, known to his friends as Poke, is a highly knowledgeable anthropologist, writer, and expert in the field of medieval demonology and secret cults. His Church of the Hermetic Science is located in Silverado, California.

Sabrina, Lady
P.O. Box 1366
Nashua, NH 03061
Tel.: 603-880-7237

Lady Sabrina is the high priestess of a coven called Our Lady of Enchantment of New Hampshire. This coven not only practices the ancient art and craft of Wicca, but also functions as a teaching coven with a very good reputation for many years.

Sintana
Tel.: 404-627-3530

Sintana (Naomi Lerman), a teacher by profession, is a knowledgeable practitioner of beneficent witchcraft, as well as a psychic and healer residing in the Atlanta vicinity.

7

ASTROLOGERS

Astrology is the art of forecasting based upon mathematical calculations of the heavens. Astrologers are not considered psychics in that the charts they cast, which are based upon specific times and the positions of planets, are interpreted according to a methodology basically adhered to by all astrologers. It is for the most part a learned craft, not to say that intuition isn't used in chart interpretation. I have included a number of astrologers whom I consider extremely adept in chart interpretation concerning the delineation of particular influences operating in a person's life. Astrologers do not necessarily predict the future; rather, they define influences in order to alert a client to circumstances that could occur in their lives so that they may better cope with the situation. The outcome depends upon the path the client chooses or his fate.

Ackerman, Shelley
Tel.: 212-539-3100

Shelley Ackerman is the host of a radio program called *Karmic Relief* and is president of the New York affiliate of the American Federation of Astrologers. She is a well-known astrologer. Shelley is the resident astrologer at the New York Theosophical Society, where she lectures and teaches. She has also written for *New Woman* magazine, *Sports Illustrated for*

Women, the *New York Daily News,* and the *New York Post.*
She has been featured on CNN, the BBC, and hundreds of
other television and radio programs in both the United States
and overseas. "My focus with astrological counseling is both
empowering and transforming," she said. "I like to combine
the mystical with the practical and give the client something
very tangible to work with. Astrology, applied correctly and
creatively, can facilitate miracles in people's lives. And it has in
my own."

Konigsberg, Patricia
Tel.: 914-679-8153

Patricia Konigsberg has been practicing astrology for thirty
years in the New York metropolitan area. Her specialty is
health, using the tools of specially created health charts and
astro-cartography. She frequently works in conjunction with
medical doctors. She is also a licensed medical massage therapist and a Jin Shia Jyutsu therapist.

Marks, Robert
Tel.: 212-535-1549

Outspoken and direct Bob Marks is one of the very best
astrologers. He has one of the longest running astrology television programs (since 1979) called *Astrology Now.* Bob practices in New York City, but can give readings by telephone.
Mr. Marks strongly feels that location influences success.

Palmer, Lynne
Tel.: 800-615-3352

Lynne Palmer is undoubtedly one of the very best astrologers
in the United States today. I have personally known Lynne for
over twenty years and wrote about her work in my book

Astrology—What It Can Do for You. Ms. Palmer is also a celebrated author with many successful books published, including *Signs for Success, Prosperity Signs, Your Lucky Days and Numbers, Money Magic,* and, the most important of all, her *Astrological Almanac for 1999.* I never make any important appointment without first consulting the latter book! Ms. Palmer

has written for many newspapers and magazines as well as appearing on many television and radio programs. She provides a wide array of astrological services, including natal charts, solar return charts, comparison charts, relationship charts, and marriage horoscopes.

Weingarten, Henry
350 Lexington Avenue
New York, NY 10016
Tel.: 212-949-7211

Henry Weingarten and the New York Astrology Center is a very important source for obtaining accurate and reliable astrological information. The center also offers the service of creating astrological charts from their computer program. Mr. Weingarten specializes in the forecasting of financial and business opportunities and published a book, *Investing by the Stars,* now in its second printing, concerning financial and business astrology; he is currently working on a second book. The center has an internationally renowned reputation as a reliable and accurate source of astrological information.

8

NUMEROLOGISTS

Closely related to astrology is the craft of numerology, which is based upon the interpretation of numbers relating to a person's life, i.e., birth dates, house numbers, etc. Numerologers also calculate the numeral equivalent of a person's name based upon a system of numerical delineation of the alphabet. Numerologers are not considered psychics in that their craft is learned; however, they can use intuition and psychic impressions when interpreting a particular situation.

Bunker, Dusty
P.O. Box 868
Exeter, NH 03833
Tel.: 603-926-8604

Dusty Bunker is the author of several fundamental books on numerology, including *Numerology and Your Future* (Schiffer, 1997). She is also a great teacher of this method of divination.

Collins, Carol
Tel.: 212-691-9848

Carol Collins is an excellent and well-respected numerologist.

Di Pietro, Sylvia

55 West 14th Street
New York, NY 10011
Tel.: 212-255-4059

Sylvia De Pietro, the author of a popular book entitled *Live Your Life by the Numbers,* has appeared on numerous programs as an expert in the field of numerology. In addition to being a professional numerologist, she also hosts a cable television program featuring various topics related to her field. She uses numerology to make predictions and suggest name changes, as well as to define many other aspects of a person's personality. Ms. Di Pietro has developed quite a following and maintains that the postal zip code of a place will also influence the area's character and future.

9

PALMISTS

An almost forgotten art of divination, palm reading has recently made a comeback since the days of carnivals and charity bazaars. With the influx of Eastern philosophy in the past twenty years, many Indian palm readers have found their way to the United States, reviving this ancient method of forecasting a person's life path.

Haas, Eric
Tel.: 212-427-3103

Eric Haas is a first-class palm reader in the New York metropolitan area. He is very good at his craft, with an excellent ability in interpretation.

APPENDIX
GROUPS AND ASSOCIATIONS

American Society for Psychical Research
5 West 73rd Street
New York, NY 10023
Tel.: 212-700-5050

Association for Research and Enlightenment
150 West 28th Street
New York, NY 10001
Tel.: 212-691-7690
Tel.: 804-428-3588 (Virginia Beach, VA, headquarters)

Better known as the Edgar Cayce Foundation, with the headquarters located in Virginia Beach, Virginia, the Association
for Research and Enlightenment sponsors lectures, seminars,
classes, and activities commensurate with the philosophy and
teachings of Edgar Cayce. The organization publishes many
books, especially on the work of the founder Edgar Cayce,
and has chapters in various cities.

California Society for Psychical Study, Inc.
P.O. Box 844
Berkeley, CA 94701

Parapsychology Foundation, Inc.
228 East 71st Street
New York, NY 10021
Tel.: 212-628-1550

The Maryland Society for Psychical Research
3365 Everly Road
Accident, MD 22150
Tel.: 301-746-6168

This society is headed by Ron and Nancy Stallings, a couple who are avid psychic investigators. Nancy is also a natural medium who has recently written a book detailing her experiences entitled *Show Me One Soul* (1997), published by Noble House.

The Metaphysical Center of New Jersey
P.O. Box 94
Bloomingdale, NJ 07403
Tel.: 973-835-7863

The Parapsychology Society of Detroit, Michigan
Tel.: 313-758-1040

This group sponsors lectures and seminars and is headed by its founder and leading spirit, businessman Lou Golden.

The United Nations Society for Parapsychology
R.S. 1755
GCPO Box 20
New York, NY 10017

This organization functions primarily for the international staff of the United Nations.

Weiser's
P.O. Box 612
York Beach, ME 03910
Tel.: 207-363-4393
Fax: 207-363-5799

This bookstore and publishing house specializes in literature on psychics, psychic phenomena, and related topics.

GLOSSARY

Many are confused about terms used in describing various aspects of the paranormal. Others do not understand the differences between certain terms such as ESP and parapsychology, medium and clairvoyant, etc. For that reason, following is a list of the most commonly used terms with their definitions. Those searching for more sophisticated *termini technici,* such as some of the East Indian words used in meditation, can find them in books specializing in the respective subdivisions, of which many are readily available today in bookstores such as East West, located in New York City in lower Manhattan.

Some of my explanations may differ from those listed in general encyclopedias and dictionaries. Early dictionaries were not particularly geared to true occult definitions, however, more recent editions have begun to redefine their terminology.

Astral Projection
Also called "out-of-body experience," this refers to the sensation of leaving the physical body, traveling at great speed to distant places, and observing various events, people, and situations. Upon return to the body, a sensation of falling from great heights is usually present, as the traveling speed of the "inner" or spiritual body is sharply reduced to fit it back into place within the slower, denser physical body. Subjects usually recall their "trip" in great detail. Astral projection can also be experimentally induced under test conditions. It is totally different from ordinary dreams in that it is a clear, precise memory of having been places. Some astral travelers are physically tired as if they had really traveled about.

Black Mass
Essentially the product of the bored upper strata of British and French society during the second half of the eighteenth century, the ceremony harkens back to the Middle Ages where it was practiced on rare occasions by anticlerical elements, and sometimes by individuals seeking power through it. During the eighteenth century, it was a fashionable thrill. It is rarely practiced today, except by individuals and groups verging on mental aberration.

It consists of a deliberate reversal of the Roman Catholic Mass, with the cross hung upside down and the litany said backward. The Black Mass is thought to mock God and Jesus Christ. Witches never practice Black Masses simply because they do not accept the existence of the Christian religion. They will not mock that which did not exist at the time their cult came into being, thousands of years before Christianity.

Clairvoyance, Clairaudience, Clairsentience
The ability to see, hear, or smell beyond the ordinary five senses. A clairvoyant person foresees events before they happen or while they happen at a distance from the clairvoyant's location. Seeing into the past is also part of this gift, as is the ability to see, hear, or smell events, people, and things not physically present but existing either in another place or on another plane of existence, such as the so-called "hereafter."

Control Personality
Trance mediums have guides, sometimes called *controls* or *control personalities*. These are individuals who have died and then attached themselves to the particular medium to help her or him. Their role is much like that of a telephone operator between worlds. Some psychiatrists feel that the controls are in reality split-off parts of the medium's own personality. However, some parapsychologists do accept the individual

existence of the controls as independent persons, especially in cases in which the control shows marked personality differences from the medium's own.

Déjà Vu

Literally "already seen," the term means the sudden, fleeting impression many people have of having been to a place, having met someone before, or having heard, seen, or done something before, which in reality they have not. For example, a soldier going overseas for the first time might recognize a certain house in a strange city as if he had been there before. Or a person might hear himself say something he knows he has said in exactly the same words before but cannot recall when.

The overwhelming number of these déjà vu flashes must be explained as precognitive flashes (*see* Precognition), that is to say, foreknowledge of the event experienced prior to the actual occurrence, but unnoticed by the person having the experience at that time. However, when the event becomes "objective reality," the fact that one is familiar with the event is realized and the precognitive flash acknowledged. A smaller percentage of déjà vu experiences, however, clearly indicate partial reincarnation memories.

Dreams

There are four types of dreams: dreams caused by physical stress, such as indigestion; dreams of psychoanalytical nature expressing suppressed emotions or desires; **astral projection** dreams; and psychic or true dreams. In the latter, the sleeper receives specific information about the future, either in the form of a warning of events to come or in the form of a scene showing the event as inevitable. Sometimes deceased individuals make contact with the sleeper in this state when his resistance to receiving communication from the beyond is lower than while fully awake.

Ectoplasm

Examined some years ago at the University of London, ectoplasm turned out to be an albumen substance related to the sexual fluids within the body and secreted by certain glands. It is present during so-called **materialization** seances and in thinner form also when apparitions occur, as well as in **poltergeist** phenomena when ectoplasm is formed to move physical objects about it. It comes from inside the body of the **medium** as well as the **sitters,** and it must be returned after the experiment to avoid damage to the health of the individuals. Ectoplasm is sensitive to white and yellow light and can exist safely only in dark red illumination.

ESP

The term was coined by Dr. Joseph B. Rhine, formerly of Duke University. Extrasensory perception, in my definition, is the obtaining of information beyond that possible by ordinary means and the five senses as we know them today. It operates through the so-called sixth sense. The latter is not a separate sense but merely the extension of the five senses beyond what we ordinarily think are their limitations, but which in fact, are not.

Neither extrasensory perception nor the sixth sense imply anything supernatural.

Ether and Etheric Body

The ether in this context is the surrounding atmosphere in the sense that it conducts psychic emanations. Thoughts travel through the ether, and apparitions of the dead exist in the etheric world. The etheric body is the finer, inner body, an exact duplicate of the grosser, outer, or physical body. At death, the etheric body assumes all functions and appearances of the physical shell.

Ghost

Ghosts are the surviving emotional memories of people who have died violently, or in some way traumatically, and who cannot leave the place of their unexpected or untimely passing. Ghosts are people with their mental faculties severely curtailed, limited to their last impulses, such as some unfinished business or complaint, and they are often unaware of their true status, that is, being outside a physical body. Ghosts neither travel from place to place nor do they normally harm anyone except through fear. The latter is unwarranted since ghosts are entirely occupied with their own problems. These visual images of dead people have been photographed under satisfactory scientific test conditions.

Glossolalia

Also called "speaking in tongues" by religiously oriented researchers, this is nothing more than the ability of trance. The voice speaking through the entranced person may speak in a language totally unknown to the speaker while in his or her conscious state, or it may even be a fantasy language.

Hypnosis

The state of detachment from the conscious self induced by verbal commands or other means, such as sound and light patterns, in which the subject will do two things: (1) reveal freely his innermost thoughts beyond what he will reveal in the conscious state for various reasons; and (2) accept suggestions he must carry out after he is returned to the normal state. Hypnosis is safe in the hands of medical doctors and of trained psychic researchers when it is also used in reincarnation experiments (*see* Regression). It is not a stage entertainment, although often used as such, and even less of a parlor game.

Incantation

In the Pagan cults, especially witchcraft, incantations are intense emotional appeals to the deity to do certain things for the petitioner. They are similar to prayers except that they are not dependent on the goodwill of the deity. Incantations always work, in the view of the Pagan believer, because they contain just the right formula, just the proper words to "make things happen."

Karma
Not merely an East Indian religious philosophy, but part of the system of reincarnation accepted equally by many in the Western world, karma is the universal law of rewards for certain actions undertaken in one lifetime but paid off in another. The individual does not generally know what his or her karma from the past consists of; the karmic law operates in the way certain opportunities arise in the present life, or in the way people meet again who may have known each other in an earlier life. What the individual does of his own free will, and from his own moral and spiritual resources, will determine the manner in which the karma is "paid off" or extinguished.

Levitation
The ability, often photographed, of physical objects, such as tables and chairs and occasionally even people, to float above the floor for a short time. This is caused by an electromagnetic force field created through the body of a powerful "physical" medium in the immediate vicinity. Great religious ecstasy has on occasion also lowered the weight of a person temporarily so that he would "float up" to the ceiling. It cannot be reproduced at will, however.

Magic(k)
The practical "arm" of witchcraft and other Pagan cults, magic, sometimes spelled with a *k* in the antiquated fashion to distinguish it from modern stage magic with which it has nothing in common, is the better and deeper understanding of the laws of nature beyond that which the average person knows, and a transforming of a reality in accordance with will. In this knowl-

edge lie answers to manipulating certain events and people that seem miraculous but are, in effect, perfectly natural.

Materialization
The rare and often imitated ability to produce ectoplasm, which in turn takes on the actual three-dimensional forms of deceased persons. Genuine materialization experiments have been conducted in England by reputable researchers, usually in rooms illuminated by adequate red light. The materialization medium usually sits in a black cabinet or closet, open on one side only, and the ectoplasm pours from the mouth and nose of the deeply entranced medium. Genuine materializations rise slowly from the floor and eventually melt back into it when the power fails. Counterfeit materializations, such as have been staged for years in American Spiritualist camps in the summer months, can be spotted fairly easily since the materialized "spirit" forms walk on and off in their full heights.

Medium
A much misunderstood term, a medium (also called a sensitive) is an intermediary, a channel between the world of the living and the world of the dead. A medium is also a person able to foretell future events and sometimes read the unknown past (*see also* Psychic). Mental mediumship includes clairvoyance, clairaudience, clairsentience, and psychometry, while physical mediumship (much rarer) consists of **trance** and **materialization.** Mediums never "summon" anyone; they merely relate what communications they receive to their clients.

Poltergeist
Formerly thought to be the product of unused sexual energies in pubescent young adults, who cause objects to fly about in

destructive ways to attract attention to themselves, the phenomena now are thought by others, including myself, to be part of ghostly manifestations. However, the unused energies of pubescent youngsters, or sometimes of retarded older people, are used by outside forces, generally deceased individuals bent on making their continued presence felt, sometimes in a malevolent fashion.

Precognition
The ability to know ahead of time events transpiring at a later date, or to know something happening a distance away without recourse to the ordinary five senses or any foreknowledge whatsoever, either conscious or unconscious.

Premonition
A vague feeling of impending events, usually destructive, sometimes specific in details, more often a general misgiving that something bad will be happening to someone, including oneself.

Psychic
The term psychic refers to the broad spectrum of all ESP phenomena, anything transcending the ordinary five senses; a psychic is a **medium.**

Psychometry
The fairly common ability to "read" past, present, or future events involving a person by touching an object owned by that person, preferably something that person alone has owned, and worn, such as a ring, a comb, or a watch. Emotional stimuli coat the object the way a thin coat of silver salts coats a photographic plate. Sensitives can reconstruct the events or read them in the future from the touch of the object.

Regression

Hypnotic regression, undertaken by qualified researchers, takes the subject in stages to his or her childhood and then cautiously past birth into an assumed earlier life. The majority of people do not recall any previous incarnation under hypnotic regression even if they consciously would like to.

A few are given to fantasizing to please the hypnotist and will create "lives" in the past. An impressive if small number of individuals have been regressed and found to have had evidential information about previous lives buried deep in their unconscious minds. All of these subjects, however, have had conscious, waking flashes of having been someone else before and were regressed only to deepen the memory of a previous incarnation, and not to find it.

Reincarnation

The conscious existence in another body and as another person, whether male or female, in a lifetime on earth prior to the present one, and the assumed continuance of that process into another life after the current reincarnation. I have documented several verified cases in *Born Again,* and Dr. Ian Stevenson has done likewise in *Twenty Cases Suggestive of Reincarnation.* Reincarnation works for everybody, but only a few can recall their previous lives, notably whose lives were cut short for one reason or another.

Satanism

The cult of worshiping the Devil principle, that is to say, human selfishness, greed, lust, and self-satisfaction. Modern Satanists, such as Anton LaVey of San Francisco's First Church of Satan, do not deny the existence of the spiritual element in man, nor the survival of human personality after death. They teach full enjoyment of the physical self, however, and are firmly opposed to charity, compassion, and other unselfish traits. True Satanists, such as exist here and there, are on the fringes of the law and sometimes involve themselves in ritual killings, usually, but not exclusively, of animals. Satanists and devil worshipers have nothing to do with witchcraft, even though they are often confused in the popular mind. Witches and Satanist are, in fact, opposites.

Seance
Actually the word means "sitting down" and refers to the assembly of several people for the purpose of spirit communication, psychic development, or other ESP research on a personal basis. Spiritualist seances often involve the holding of hands to create a "circle of power" for a few moments, or the singing of religious hymns to raise the **vibrations.** Seances can take place in the daytime or at night and are usually held in subdued light. Only in materialization seances do "spirits" appear or objects move. Most seances are for verbal communication only, through the mouth of the medium at the head of the table.

Sensitive
The same as medium or being a psychic.

Sitting and Sitter
Sitting is a more appropriate term for seance, and a sitter is a person taking part in a sitting, or someone consulting a medium privately and individually.

Spell
A spell is a prayer with the force of a directive used in witchcraft and other pagan cults to influence an event or to make certain things happen to another person not present when the spell is cast. The specific choice of words, certain ritual actions, and other aids are required to make the spell effective.

Spirit

The "inner self," that which survives physical death of the body. The spirit must not be confused with a ghost, which is an earth-bound spirit unable to move on into what Dr. Joseph B. Rhine has called the world of the mind. Spirits are free to come and go; they inhabit the world next to ours in which thoughts are instant action. Spirits are electromagnetic fields formed in the exact duplicate of the person's physical self prior to death, but usually returned to his or her prime state. Thus spirits, when they appear to the living, usually show themselves in their best years, although they are able to control their appearances at will, being thought forms only.

Spiritualism

A religion of Christian moral based upon the findings of psychic research and the belief in continuance of life in "summerland." Founded in the 1860s in America and popular also in Great Britain, Spiritualism still flourishes in many subdivisions and sects and is a recognized form of religion. It should not be confused with psychic research or parapsychlogy, however.

Telekinesis and Teleportation

The movement of solid objects by power of mind. This has been done in laboratory experiments at Duke University and recently in Soviet Russia, where it was also recorded photographically. The energy streaming out of the medium's body causes the objects to move. Teleportation is much rarer and less well documented. It involves the sudden and dramatic transportation of solid objects great distances and sometimes *through* solid objects, utilizing techniques of dematerialization and rematerialization not yet fully understood.

Trance

A state in which the medium's own personality is temporarily set aside and the spirit or personality of another person is allowed to enter the medium's body and operate the speech mechanism, vocal cords, facial muscles, etc., the way a driver operates an automobile. The driver is not the car, and the medium is not the entity speaking through her. Afterwards, the medium does not recall her actions or words while in possession by another being. Trance should only be undertaken in the presence of and under the supervision of a trained psychic researcher.

Transmigration
An East Indian belief that reincarnation is possible between humans and animals. For the present, no evidence for this exists.

Vibrations
Also called "vibes," these are movements of emotionally charged particles filling the **ether** in which we exist. They manifest themselves as emanations, rays, impressions, electromagnetic energy patterns, and so on.

Vision
A visual experience concerning events not visible to the eye at the place and time where it occurs. Swedenborg had a vision of the Stockholm fire while a day's journey away. Some visions pertain to future events also.

Witchcraft
Anglo-Saxon/Celtic witchcraft, called "Wicca," or "Craft of the Wise," is also known as "the Old Religion" by its followers. It is a true nature religion based upon three important elements:

1. The firm conviction that reincarnation is a fact and that the cycle of life continues beyond death.

2. The belief in the powers of magic, the better utilization of natural law, to make certain things happen that ordinary people are unable to accomplish.

3. The worship of the "Mother Goddess" principle of a female deity, representing the creative element in nature, thus free from original sin, guilt, shame, and anything restricting oneself to the narrow limits of an artificially motivated society. "An' it harm none, do what thou wilt," is the *sole* law of Wicca.

Index of Professionals

Psychics in the United States

Anderson, Marisa
Appio, Carol Ann
Bard, Ronald
Baron-Reid, Colette
Bassik, Susan
Cattel
Char
Craig, Pat
Daryl, Jason (Lundstead)
Deitch, Paula
De La Rochelle, Lyn
De Long, Barbara
DeLouise, Joseph
Doherty, Jane
Downey, Jim
Dratler, Theresa
Dykshoorn, M. B.
Esposito, Peggy
Fahrusha (Roseanne Shaffer)
Herald, Joy

Hoffman, Judy
Hughes, Irene
Jaegers, Beverly
Joyce, Elizabeth
Karter, Kathleen
Levy, Elizabeth A.
McAlester, Colette
Moreno, Maria
Morton, Pat
O'Dell, Allison
Palmer, Salina
Papapetros, Maria
Paretti, Catherine
Parker, Stephen T.
Peters, Soni L.
Pignatelli, Anni
Popper, Lyn
Rivera, Lucy
Roberta
Rogers, Rosanna

Schuler, Carol
Sherman, Johanna
Sisson, Pat
Taylor, Valerie Svolos

Wagner, Chuck
Winner, Joyce
Yolana

Psychics Overseas

Al Huneidi, Sahar H.
Gardner, Richard
Gaudy, John
Hearne, Ronald

Montgomery, Pauline
  (Maddock)
Solomon, Philip
Van Der Heide, Jan
  Cornelius

Healers

Bernardo, Cesar
Blake, Mary
Collins, Doris
Cooper, Maria
Dye, Betty
Guidice, Lena
Healing Light Center

Kolman, Ze've
Kraft, Dean
Krystal, Phyllis
Lucas, Heidi
Poyel, Elaine
Purpora, Maureen

Pagans and Witches

Adams, Frederick
  McLauren
de Arechaga, Frederick
  (Ordun)
Curott, Phyllis

Enchantments
Morgana
Runyon, Carroll
Sabrina, Lady
Sintana

Astrologers

Ackerman, Shelley
Konigsberg, Patricia
Marks, Robert

Palmer, Lynne
Weingarten, Henry

NUMEROLOGISTS

Bunker, Dusty
Collins, Carol

DiPietro, Sylvia

PALMISTS

Haas, Eric

ABOUT THE AUTHOR

Hans Holzer, Ph.D., is the author of 131 books including *Ghosts, ESP and You, The Handbook of Parapsychology, The Power of Hypnosis, Are You Psychic?* and *Life Beyond.* He taught parapsychology for eight years at the New York Institute of Technology, and was educated at Columbia University, the University of Vienna, and received a doctorate from the London College of Applied Science.

Dr. Holzer has also been an active television and film writer, producer, and on camera person, notably for the NBC series *In Search of...* and half a dozen documentaries. He has surveyed the psychic scene, and developed a number of gifted psychics for many years. He makes his home in New York City.